GW00775854

EVEntful Years

Also available in this series:

Fred Archer	BENEDICT'S POOL
Peter Austen	THE COUNTRY ANTIQUE DEALER
Mary Barnard	THE DIARY OF AN OPTIMIST
Pip Beck	A WAAF IN BOMBER COMMAND
Adrian Bell	THE CHERRY TREE
Mary Sydney Burke	THE SOLDIER'S WIFE
Jennifer Davies	TALES OF THE OLD GYPSIES
Roger Hutchings	CRYSTAL PALACE VISTAS
Ken Hankins	A CHILD OF THE THIRTIES
Herbert C. Harrison	THE MILL HOUSE AND THEREABOUTS
Gregory Holyoake	THE PREFAB KID
Erma Harvey James	WITH MAGIC IN MY EYES
Joy Lakeman	THEM DAYS
Len Langrick	SNOWBALL: GO FIND YOURSELF A SCHOOL
Florence Mary McDowell	OTHER DAYS AROUND ME
Madeline MacDonald	THE LAST YEAR OF THE GANG
Angela Mack	DANCING ON THE WAVES
Brian P. Martin	TALES FROM THE COUNTRY PUB
Roger Mason	GRANNY'S VILLAGE
Cicely Mayhew	BEADS ON A STRING
Christian Miller	A CHILDHOOD IN SCOTLAND
Katharine Moore	QUEEN VICTORIA IS VERY ILL
J. C. Morten and Sheila Morten	I REMAIN, YOUR SON JACK
Pauline Neville	PEGGY
Humphrey Phelps	JUST ACROSS THE FIELDS
Angela Raby	THE FORGOTTEN SERVICE
Phyl Surman	PRIDE OF THE MORNING
Doreen Louie West	LOUIE: AN OXFORD LADY
Elizabeth West	HOVEL IN THE HILLS
Hazel Wheeler	HALF A POUND OF TUPPENNY RICE
William Woodrow	ANOTHER TIME, ANOTHER PLACE

EVEntful Years

CONTINUING THE MEMORIES OF "ADAMANT EVE"

1948-1955

Eve Day

ISIS
LARGE PRINT
Oxford

First published in Great Britain 2000
by Eve Day

Published in Large Print 2002 by ISIS Publishing Ltd,
7 Centremead, Osney Mead, Oxford OX2 0ES
by arrangement with Eve Day

British Library Cataloguing in Publication Data
Day, Eve
    Eventful Years : continuing the memories of "Adamant Eve"
    1948-1955. - Large print ed.
    1.Day, Eve 2.Large type books 3.Great Britain - Social life
    and customs - 1945- 4.Great Britain - Biography
    I.Title
    941 .0854'092

            ISBN 0-7531-9754-5 (hb)
            ISBN 0-7531-9755-3 (pb)

Printed and bound by Antony Rowe, Chippenham

For all my dear friends who enjoyed "Adamant Eve" and encouraged me to tell them what happened next.

I've always liked to rhyme, I do it all the time.
To write a book and overlook this chance, 'twould be a crime!

Acknowledgement

My sincere thanks to Kath Keating for her
helpfulness and advice.

To Erica Gamble for her patience and expertise in
typing this manuscript.

Also to Kelmscott Library "Come Write In" writers'
group for their nurture and encouragement.

"Our lives are like identical suitcases, some of us
manage to pack more into them than others."

CONTENTS

1. Chapter One   1
2. Chapter Two   8
3. Chapter Three   16
4. Chapter Four   25
5. Chapter Five   31
6. Chapter Six   40
7. Chapter Seven   47
8. Chapter Eight   55
9. Chapter Nine   59
10. Chapter Ten   67
11. Chapter Eleven   73
12. Chapter Twelve   79
13. Chapter Thirteen   82
14. Chapter Fourteen   87
15. Chapter Fifteen   93
16. Chapter Sixteen   99
17. Chapter Seventeen 104
18. Chapter Eighteen   107
19. Chapter Nineteen   111

FOREWORD

"EVEntful Years" chronicles that euphoric time when a young woman, free as an emergent butterfly, sheds the cocoon of school uniform. Life options bloom as roses and our butterfly chooses those on which to alight or fly over.

Eve captures this sense of freedom and excitement well, and as a bonus, grants us an almost unintentional yet valuable commentary on rapid social and economic change in post war England. It became no longer sufficient to be purely decorative. A butterfly earned her wings as surely and bravely as any fabled air ace.

Kath Keating

CHAPTER
ONE

At Oakwood with the babies, I tucked them in their prams.
I studied hard at Tech, so that I coped with my exams.

Rebellion has never been in my nature, but that is how
my father saw it when I told him I was leaving school
before my final year, as I had a job.

"How will you support yourself?" he enquired
testily.

"I'll manage somehow," was my adamant reply.
Dad doubted my ability to cope with living on a **very**
limited income, but I had a stubborn streak and made
up my mind I would succeed in my chosen career.
Occasionally I regret not having completed that final
year and then attended the Teachers' Training College
that had already interviewed me. What would life have
offered me had I followed that path, who knows? As it
is I am grateful to have enjoyed the rich experiences
and many facets of various occupations.
The first day at Oakwood Day Nursery in Guildford
Surrey, remains vividly in my mind. Matron Catherine
Sutherland, referred to by the staff as "Katie",
welcomed me then escorted me on a tour of the
building. Originally a large country house with lawns

1

sweeping down to the tranquil River Wey, it had been converted for use as a Day Nursery and residence. Trudi the cook lived in a bed-sitting room in the attic and Matron occupied the private wing on the first floor with her eight year old son Iain.

"Cyclops Iain," she reminded us, "with an 'I' in the middle!" referring of course to the spelling of his name. I loved that explanation and have a couple of relatives whose daughters are "Cyclops Claire"!

First we climbed the staircase to the first floor where the babies' nursery with its large shaded balcony overlooked the colourful gardens. The cots could be wheeled on to this area during wet or stormy weather. Fresh air, irrespective of the temperature, was considered vital. Providing it was not actually raining or snowing, we carried the babies downstairs wrapped up warmly and tucked them into their prams. There they lay under the trees mesmerised by the patterns of the quivering leaves until they slept peacefully. Adjacent to the nursery stood the bathroom, lavatory and babies' food preparation room.

"Aren't they gorgeous!" I admired the tiny infants in the rows of cots.

"Yes, they are," agreed Matron, "but a great deal of work is involved to keep them clean and contented, you have a lot to learn. Now let us have a look downstairs at the other groups."

To the left of the imposing entrance hall, Matron's office was a reminder of all the administrative needs of such an establishment. Nearby, the staff room doubling as our dining room, looked comfortable and bright. Matron loved colour. Friezes of nursery characters decorated the walls of the tweenies' nursery, painted some years previously by "Big Mary" the staff nurse. The "tweenies" were aged from about one year to eighteen months and the "toddlers" eighteen months to two years old.

Some of these little ones were quite steady on their feet but many found crawling much quicker. Ann entertained a small enthusiastic group playing

"Pat a cake, pat a cake, baker's man
Bake me a cake as fast as you can.
Pat it and prick it and mark it with 'B'
And put in the oven for baby and me."

The children's bathroom with two low hand basins and miniature lavatories adjoined the staff bathroom. In the laundry we dealt with washing endless nappies, bibs and soiled clothes and bedding. No disposable nappies in those days, or washing machines. We used a glass wash board and a large copper to boil the clothes. Drying them on rainy days caused problems. Matron did not approve, but when we found ourselves desperate for items, we spread the nappies on airers in the boiler room.

Before showing me the toddlers' room which like the tweenies', had French doors opening on to a patio and the gardens, we had a vital procedure to perform. Entering the neat linen room, Matron found three green overalls my size which became my daily uniform for the duration of my two year training. She then entrusted me to Mary's tender care and tuition for the next three months.

The babies' feeds were prepared four hourly and we were taught to make the formulas and sterilise the bottles. We accomplished this in a formidable looking, temperamental steel steriliser in which they were boiled. Mary, a tall, well built, warm hearted blonde did not believe in allowing babies to distress themselves by crying, although feeding times were rigid.

"Cuddle them, talk to them and play with them," she encouraged us. I loved their responsiveness and happily played

> "This little piggy went to market,
> This little piggy stayed at home,
> This little piggy had roast beef,
> This little piggy had none,
> And THIS little piggy went wee wee wee
> all the way home."

with their tiny toes.

My worst experience at the Day Nursery happened during my first month. The tray stood on the low table as we fed the babies. It contained a bottle of Cod Liver oil, for Vitamin D, a bottle of the sweet, sticky Government subsidised orange juice, for Vitamin C, zinc and caster oil "bottom" cream and a jar of cotton wool swabs. I carried it carefully into the nursery after cleaning it, tripped and the whole lot came crashing down. Splinters of glass flew everywhere and a horrific mess of variegated fluids oozed on to the polished parquet flooring.

"Ooo I'm sorry, I'm sorry," I stammered, trying to retrieve shards of glass as the blood from cuts on my leg added to the chaotic mess.

"Are you all right?" Mary ever solicitous did not chastise me then but I had a severe scolding later from Matron for my clumsiness. After that disaster I treated all trays with the greatest respect. It was not long after the war and many commodities were difficult to obtain so we avoided any waste. The shame and mortification I felt is something that remains with me still.

Many of the babies took their first faltering steps whilst with us. We never told their mothers, leaving this delightful milestone as a surprise for her to discover.

After my fragmented childhood spent in so many schools and foster homes, the Maloney family had given me a degree of stability. Now that I was earning, it was I who paid to board with them instead of Dad. I would have liked to be more independent now that I was eighteen, but with such limited money it seemed I was doomed to remain a dependant of the family for some time.

The other staff at the Day Nursery in hierarchical order after Matron and Staff Nurse, were Jane, in charge of the "tweenies", Elaine with the toddlers, the three student nursery nurses, Ann, Avona and myself. Connie and little Mary acted as nursery maids. The only bickering was between the latter two girls. They both fancied Peter, one of the men who maintained and hired out rowing boats on the river.

Our favourite walk took us past the boathouse, along the riverbank. I pushed the heavy, deep old pram up the steep slopes with a child sitting at each end. A toddler on reins tugged at each side of me. In this way four of us gave sixteen children a little excursion. Sometimes we wandered through some of the quaint old cobbled streets of that very ancient town dominated by the Keep of Guildford castle. This dated from the twelfth century being built by King Henry II. This infamous king was responsible for the martyrdom of Archbishop Thomas à Becket.

The course to become a registered Nursery Nurse took two years. Three days each week I enjoyed the practical experience at the Day Nursery and later at the Nursery School for the two, three and four year olds. Two days a week I attended Guildford Technical College. Unlike many of the other students, I had a good School Certificate plus a year towards the Higher School Certificate, so academically I coped well with subjects such as English and Maths. At school I never had the opportunity to learn any science so hygiene, food and nutrition and child development were new to me. I certainly enjoyed studying these subjects.

"Elmdon", an old house adjacent to the Technical College housed the Nursery Nurses' course plus some of the science subjects. Many a time we arrived to gasp at graphic anatomical diagrams on the blackboard. In my second year I won a prize for designing a nursery school based on the letter "E". The three wings for each nursery having access to covered play areas and the business and recreational parts, the stalk of the "E". Malcolm, my neighbour at the time, a student architect, helped me to produce the impressive plans.

Over the whole course I came second. This is the story of my life! I lacked ambition and could have probably come first but never had that competitive drive to excel. The most important aim was to pass my exam and be able to write "N.N.E.B." after my name — National Nursery Examination Board. The course was established in 1946 and I commenced in 1948.

Most of the students arrived by buses from outlying towns or country districts. Here many were employed in residential institutions such as church run orphanages or Dr Barnardo's Homes. The children in these situations were adequately fed and cared for but their lifestyle was definitely institutionalised. Many were abandoned, orphaned or illegitimate. To be an unmarried mother in those days was the ultimate disgrace.

CHAPTER
TWO

To leave Maloneys AND return was never my intention. Enter boys! Then my life took on a new dimension.

My method of transport, my elderly B.S.A. bicycle, had belonged to cousin Jill. Fortunately I lived near enough to work and Tech to cycle each day. Luckily my work overalls were provided as I had little money to spare. Out of my weekly wage of one pound sixteen shillings, Mrs Maloney took thirty shillings for my keep and three shillings covered the price of our lunches at the nursery. Three shillings were left for my clothing, occasional bus and train fares and entertainment. Because of these circumstances my social life had been nil.

This changed dramatically the day Connie and Mary persuaded me to join Shalford Youth Club. They both lived in outlying villages and travelled to Guildford daily by bus. Connie's parents had a small farm cottage and a large family. Her father worked as a cowman. Mary's father had the prestigious job of village blacksmith.

Shalford was a pretty village only a few miles from Guildford. Our youth club leader, David Dunhill, was a BBC presenter. As well as being a newsreader, he introduced the popular radio show "Take It From Here", written by Frank Muir and Denis Norden. The producer Charles Maxwell, initially brought this talented pair together. This starred Jimmy Edwards, Dick Bentley and Alma Cogan. June Whitfield took over from Alma Cogan later. "The Glums", Ron, Eth and Mr Glum portrayed a true-to-life family. Their engagement seemed permanent to Eth's frustration. "Oh RON!"

Occasionally David gave a few of us tickets to watch the show as it was being broadcast; a fascinating experience. These talented comedians gave us a taste of what was to come as a "warm up". When I hear audience laughter at unexpected places on radio programmes, I realise a lot of the clowning is not audible!

Sometimes I babysat for the Dunhills' little girl Vanessa in their lovely home. This welcome extra money enabled me to get a cheap day return from Guildford to Waterloo station for a day in London. As I had been born and spent quite a bit of my childhood in the City, I capably travelled by bus or tube and knew my way around the great Metropolis.

The youth club being "mixed" I met BOYS for the first time in my very sheltered life. I liked them! I hadn't realised what I had been missing, and have enjoyed male company ever since. Physiologically a very early developer, psychologically due to circumstances, my hormones had been kept subdued. Enter Malcolm and Nick! These inseparable friends were two stunning looking boys. Malcolm had blue eyes, was tall with curly blond hair but it was Nick's grey eyes, dark hair and beguiling smile that enchanted me. He had recently left Cranleigh School, a boys' public school. Now he was intended to be a partner in his father's oil heating business in Kingsway, Central London. Nick loved to write and eventually became a prestigious medical journalist.

Recently I heard of a small boy asking, "Mummy what is a rapist?"

She was very disconcerted and said "Why are you asking that, Ben?" "Well," he replied, "there was a sign outside that house that said "PHYSIO THE RAPIST"!

Nick and I occasionally made up a foursome with Malcolm and his girlfriend Betsy. An attractive girl with a shapely figure, she was training to be a physiotherapist. Later I heard this story, which I believe is fact. Malcolm and Betsy married and had a family. She worked privately for an agency that had some very rich clients. One older man found her very attractive, and I gather she left Malcolm and the children who were almost grown up and lived with him in the south of France. Not for long though, he died and left her the villa. She returned to Malcolm, he moved in too, and as far as I know they're living happily there. The wages of sin?!

Suddenly I found myself in love. Tuesday evenings, youth club night, took on a special enchantment. I could hardly believe that my feelings were reciprocated but soon Nick and I were "going out together".

My life now revolved around Saturdays when we met and Tuesday evenings. We went for long walks in the beautiful countryside. Occasionally a good film lured us to the cinema. Nick taught me to play Canasta and gave me a set as a gift, which I still have. Danny Kaye was a favourite of mine. Nick bought me a "singles" record of him singing the popular song "The Peony Bush". When I told his mother the title, I remember her asking

"Do WHAT in a bush?!"

Nick's parents had a large charming house in Shalford. His younger brother sported the unusual but rather attractive names of Ambrose Peregrine. A kind elderly lady, his mother's nanny who had also been Nick's nanny, resided there permanently, devoted to the family. (One thing that made a lasting impression on me was the full size bookcase that resided in their downstairs lavatory, the ultimate luxury!)

Then misfortune struck. He was conscripted to do his two years compulsory National Service. He joined the Royal Engineers and our meetings were necessarily curtailed. He was stationed not too far away and came home on occasional leave, looking very dashing in his uniform. In between, we wrote each other long, loving letters. An incurable romantic, I longed to be with him; if that was not possible, gloat over his wonderfully written letters — and if all else failed, just gaze at his home.

I left the Maloneys and moved in right opposite Nick's house. The Veit family needed someone as an "au pair" to help with the children and some household tasks. I still cycled to work and Tech but was available on demand to babysit. Their eldest boy David boarded at his public school. Robin aged eight went daily to a local preparatory school and little Mark aged four was at home. This charming family were very kind to me and I enjoyed my time there. For the first time in my life I was able to start my lifelong habit of saving a proportion of my wages, as I lived there rent free.

The boys all spoke with a very refined accent. I naturally spent a lot of time with Mark, a highly intelligent little boy who was always asking questions.

"Tell me, Eve," he said one day as I bathed him, "when I faht in the bahth, why does it make bubbles?"

The next day we had technical explanations with a funnel, tube and a bowl of water. This pertinent remark has been a catchphrase in my family ever since.

My poor bike that I tended carefully really needed a "face-lift". Malcolm, a keen cyclist, fixed the brakes and put on new tyres then offered to paint it silver. He had a can of paint in a spray. Mark, Robin and a couple of their little friends watched entranced as my dowdy bike was transformed. The other outcome of this incident was that four small children ended up with silver toe caps to their shoes!

I still attended the youth club and their dramatic group, acting Mrs White in "The Monkey's Paw" by W. W. Jacobs, ably produced by David.

The popular songs of the time had us all singing

"Put another nickel in,
in the nickelodeon,
all I want is loving you and
music — music — music," and

"Fairy tales can come true,
it can happen to you, if you're young at heart!"

Each Sunday, as I had through all my teenage years during the school holidays, I met my father at Lyons restaurant in the cobbled High Street. Sometimes on a Saturday I'd call in the jewellers shop "Walter Joseph" owned by his sister, my Aunt Bess, widow of Walter Joseph. She now resided in Eastbourne, married again to Uncle Bob, a handsome, successful Canadian doctor. Dad's brother Uncle Manny, a jeweller and silversmith by trade, managed these fascinating, gloomy premises. The three gold balls on the sign outside signified that they were also pawnbrokers. Dad, long since retired, helped in the shop each day. During the war I had often accompanied Uncle Manny to auctions in some of the imposing country homes in the surrounding area. I can't remember how we got there, by bus I expect, as I knew no one who had a car in those days except Uncle Harry.

Whilst I worked in Guildford, the Repertory Theatre company often borrowed silver candelabra and other items for their props, particularly for Oscar Wilde's plays such as "The Importance of Being Earnest".

In return, Uncle Manny was given a couple of the best seats in the theatre. He, or more often Dad, took me with him. This was the old theatre in North Street before the prestigious new Yvonne Arnaud Theatre was built on the river bank, named after the famous actress. Sometimes they had a Music Hall there with visiting artistes, many of whom later became famous. Dad instilled in me a love of the old Music Hall songs.

"Oh I do like to be beside the seaside,
Oh I do like to be beside the sea.
Oh I do like to stroll along the prom, prom, prom,
Where the brass band plays tiddly-om-pom-pom.
Oh I do like to be beside the seaside,
I'll be beside myself with glee.
There are lots of girls beside,
I would like to be beside
Beside the seaside, beside the sea."

Nick, who definitely seemed officer material, failed his "W.O.S.B.E." (War Office Selection Board Examination) and his mother blamed me.

"He has spent too much time and attention on you when he should have been preparing for this exam."

She was also very concerned that our relationship showed signs of becoming serious. I had always had a great respect and fear of authority and she was a powerful character. Her severe lecture had me totally intimidated.

"You should leave the Veits'," she demanded, "for the sake of Nick's future."

"Where shall I go?" I pleaded with her.

"Back to the Maloneys", she suggested, so I packed my small suitcase that contained all I possessed and returned to the Maloneys and to complete the last phase of my training.

I felt very dejected as well as rejected and wondered if my Jewish background may have been part of her reasons for disapproval. My religion was never discussed, but also never denied. At this stage of my life I still hoped to be received into the Roman Catholic Church ONE day. I didn't come from a "good" family which is what she would have wanted for her sons. As it happened, Ambrose married a farmworker's pretty young daughter Margaret. I'm sure not his mother's choice!

CHAPTER
THREE

With the toddlers and the tweenies I learned many a new skill.
I transferred to the Nursery School, employed at Shepherds Hill.

Once the babies took their first tottering steps or
reached their first birthday, they were transferred to
the "tweenies" nursery. Here we encouraged their
newly discovered mobility with toys such as push along
trucks and sturdy wooden dolls' prams. The most
popular toy was two strong boxes. One we filled with
items such as blocks, spoons, small balls and wooden
bobbins. The other box was empty. I remember little
Freda's screams of delight as she took each item out of
one box to drop it in the other with a satisfying "plop".
One frequent problem was "Puss", the gentle,
amenable black and white cat who could not resist an
empty box and did not take kindly to being pelted with
blocks.

We sang   "I love little pussy
             Her coat is so warm.
             And if I don't hurt her
             She'll do me no harm.
             So I'll not pull her tail,

Nor drive her away,
But pussy and I
Very gently will play."

Trudi, the excellent Austrian cook prepared a substantial lunch daily for the staff. In those days the custom was to have one's main meal at midday and a "high tea" in the late afternoon/early evening. The children had their lunch seated at low tables. Mealtimes were mildly chaotic. I sat with one "tweenie" on each side of me shovelling food into open mouths like a mother bird attending her fledglings. We encouraged independence so the more able ones and toddlers fed themselves or tipped the food on to the floor or over each other.

"William, try to use your spoon, not your fingers."

"Jeremy, your food bowl belongs on the table, not on your head."

"Oh Gillian, Puss doesn't want your dinner thrown at her."

After they finished their meal, nappies were changed, bibs removed and the children lay on little stretcher beds to rest for an hour or two. While they hopefully slept, we had a three quarters of an hour break, in two shifts for our lunch. Most of these little ones were well ready for a snooze after an active morning. Because the mothers needed to get to work on time, some had been woken very early. Sandra fought sleep. She fidgeted, cried, got more irritable and naughty the more tired she became. Sometimes they called me from the staff room in desperation as she disturbed the more amenable children.

"Come and do your hypnotism, Eve," they begged.

I sat by her, tucking the blanket firmly around her and hummed tunelessly with constant eye contact. Slowly MY eyelids began to droop, after a brief period hers follow suit, within a few minutes she slept soundly. Later we had a singing session with simple rhymes for their developing speech.

> "One, two, three, four
> Mary at the cottage door,
> Five, six, seven, eight
> Eating cherries off the plate."

They loved that very male chauvinist song —

> "Clap hands, clap hands
> Till Daddy comes home.
> For Daddy has money
> But Mummy has none."

Times were rapidly changing. During the war women had been needed in factories, shops and taking over many roles as the men were conscripted. They enjoyed their new found financial independence. Many continued in employment, but some jobs were not available once one married.

Everything was biased to the male employee. One woman who trained as a welder during the war and became very competent was dismissed with the words — "Sorry you're redundant," no explanations. Brute force no longer being needed in the burgeoning engineering and electrical industries, women WERE employed as they were seen as cheap labour for mindless repetitive work.

Women were often thought of as temporary employees, in and out of the labour market and not expected to stick at a job. For this reason promotion went automatically to the men.

Before the war only about ten per cent of women worked but after, it rose to twenty two per cent. Feminism was epitomised by the vision of the emancipated women with horn-rimmed spectacles, hair severely in a bun and wearing a tweed suit. (Memories of some of my teachers, in particular dear Miss Dutton from Seaford.) They were getting fed up with their lower pay. Three specific groups; teachers, civil servants and local government employees started campaigning for equal pay in 1951. It took four years for a limited victory. 1955 saw phased-in payments to bring pay to the same level as the men. (This did NOT apply to nursing which was seen as women's work.)

On the whole the Women's Movement was quiet in the 1950s and women concentrated on family life. Man was the breadwinner, woman the dependent wife.

The day I transferred to the toddlers' room held many sad memories for me. One of our "tweenies", a delightful tot called Felicity, had died tragically in a house fire whilst her parents were out. I never found out if she had been alone or what caused the fire. I know it made a big impact on all of us. No counsellors in those days!

I delighted in the toddlers. Their enthusiastic involvement I found stimulating and sometimes exasperating. Curious about everything and eager to participate, Tommy loved noise. I must admit he was a favourite of mine. His blue, blue eyes, dark curls and beguiling smile charmed us all. He banged happily with a spoon on an old tin as we played nursery rhymes on the worn seventy eight rev. records. His favourite and mine was —

> "This is the way the ladies ride
> Gall-op, gall-op, gall-op, gall-op
> This is the way the ladies ride
> Gall-op, gall-op, gall-op.

Then slower
> This is the way the farmer rides,
> Cal-ump, cal-ump, cal-ump, cal-ump
> This is the way the farmer rides
> Cal-ump, cal-ump, cal-ump.

Then very slowly

> "This is the way the old men ride,
> Hobble-dee, hobble-dee, hobble-dee
> DOWN into a ditch."

Tommy enjoyed sitting on my lap facing me, jigging up and down as if riding a horse. At "down into a ditch" there would be a delighted giggle of anticipation, as I separated my legs and held his hands tightly as he fell into the "ditch". The gramophone needed winding regularly or the music subsided with a dying groan. Many years later, this game was enjoyed by my own children and grandchildren.

It was Tommy who one day proudly showed his potty to an audience of very interested toddlers. Its contents were a surprising shade of red. After the initial alarm, we remembered that he had enjoyed a second helping of beetroot the previous day!

In order to gain some practical experience with the two to five year olds, I spent some time at Shepherds Hill Nursery School, the other side of Guildford. My trusty bike remained my only mode of transport.

The buildings there were purpose built, single storey and prefabricated. The three nurseries were for the two-three, three-four and four-five year olds with a communal play area. The children spent all day there, from 9.00a.m. to 4.00p.m., having their lunch, mid-morning and afternoon snack and an after lunch sleep. From one until two o'clock, three staff members who had already had their lunch hour supervised sixty children who were meant to be resting, whilst the rest of the staff had their lunch hour. We played records of classical music on the electric record player, a great improvement on the old wind up one at the Day Nursery. The idea was that it would encourage the restless ones to sleep. The younger children usually complied, but the older ones fidgeted and were often too lively to settle. They quietly looked at books.

Mrs Hammond, the headmistress, sat in her office most of the time, presumably dealing with the administration. The cook, Mrs Armstrong, loved the children and often happily allowed them to assist her. Uneven tarts and biscuits cut out with a medicine glass delighted the youngsters who were still at that charming age where they loved to help.

Each group had a trained teacher, an assistant and a student. Although the day was long, it had school holidays, unlike the Day Nursery. Then we returned to Oakwood and the under two's. I spent time in all three rooms and each one I enjoyed more than the previous one. We had a little three year old boy, Allan, whose eyes didn't focus properly and ALWAYS wore a helmet, an unusual sight in those days, as he had a huge head. He suffered from hydrocephalus — water on the brain, which caused a degree of mental retardation. Because of his abnormal weight distribution, he was always falling over. He rarely complained as the water pressed on his sensory nerves and he did not feel pain.

His frail pale faced mother came one day to explain his absence.

"Oh dear, poor Allan," she announced, "he is in hospital being treated for severe burns on his hand. I smelt something acrid and found he had placed his palm against the bars of the electric fire; it was his flesh burning."

We comforted her. Allan returned some days later proudly sporting a heavily bandaged hand which eventually healed, but left horrific scars.

Once, when I was the last on duty, in charge of locking the building and the gates, little Eileen's father arrived.

"Did Bruce collect her this afternoon after school?"

"I don't know," I replied, "she was in with the four year olds."

"I know Bruce plays around on the way home but neither of them have returned."

Just then his distraught wife arrived.

"Are they home, Gladys?" he asked.

"No, Bruce said she wasn't waiting and thought I'd collected her."

I tried not to panic. I asked them into the office and phoned Mrs Hammond who lived nearby. No, she couldn't remember Eileen going.

"I'll come straight round," she reassured me. In those days few people had telephones so I rode my bike to some of Eileen's friends' parents, in case she had gone with them. Reluctantly, Mrs Hammond phoned the police. It was then, in the deserted building, that we heard remote thumps and sounds. I looked in the four year old room and the cupboards, no sign. Then I had an idea.

"I'll have a look in the shelter. I saw her helping Mrs Clarke pack away the outside toys."

An obsolete air raid shelter served as a large storage shed. As we neared the outbuilding we could hear the distraught cries and thumping from within. We unlatched the door and there was a red eyed, frightened little girl.

"Daddy, Daddy," she cried, running eagerly into the arms of her relieved father.

One of the many rhymes the children and I enjoyed was:

"One misty, moisty morning when cloudy was the weather,
I met a little old man cloth-ed all in leather.
He began to compliment and I began to grin,
'How d'you do and how d'you do and how d'you do agin.'"

Nigel, a precocious little boy, asked what a compliment was.

"It is something you give people," I answered.

He immediately replied, "Can I have one?"

"Certainly, you're an intelligent little boy."

That required more explanation, but he soon understood the meaning of a new long word and greeted his doting mother with

"I've got a compliment for you."

"WHAT did you say?" she exclaimed.

"You are wearing a pretty frock today!"

From that day onwards he always found a compliment for me, if it was only to say he liked my white teeth.

CHAPTER
FOUR

My training now completed, new options I explored.
Nursing was my new career, the Isolation ward.

Nick's mother's chastisement and his involvement in
the army now meant we saw little of each other. I knew
I was not good enough for him but was heartbroken
that our friendship was waning. Even though we both
soon had new friends we kept in touch and his parents
were exceptionally kind to me a few years later when I
married, probably out of gratitude that it was not
to THEIR son, although by then Nick had already
married Elizabeth.

I achieved my "N.N.E.B." in December 1950 and
then had to decide my future. Did I want to apply as a
Staff Nurse at one of the residential homes? Definitely
not, I had spent too much of my life receiving
discipline and the institutional life of boarding school.
Since my eldest brother's death in 1940 and my
mother's the following year, my brother David was
my only near relative other than my rather remote and
very reserved father. We had been bombed during the
Blitz and rehoused in a flat near London Zoo.
After mother's untimely death when I was eleven, Dad

moved to a boarding house in Guildford, Surrey. Here the other boarders were young law students studying at the local law school which is why he found alternative accommodation for his nubile young daughter.

My dysfunctional childhood had consisted of having twelve changes of schools and boarding with as many different families. My lack of security during these years was fortunately compensated by a necessarily independent spirit.

David had been demobbed from the Air Force where he had been flying Spitfires and achieved the rank of Flight Lieutenant. He had no other qualifications, he just loved flying. He also loved Dorothy. His best friend in the R.A.F., Jack, married Joan, Dorothy's sister, and David found a job with a two year contract to enable him to follow Dorothy's family to New Zealand where they had emigrated. When his contract expired he happily returned to flying. He married Dorothy, had three sons and they lived happily ever after!

I loved David dearly. My romance was over, so why not try to join him in New Zealand? I sent for the literature for an assisted passage, and perused the list of desired occupations. One in particular appealed to me, Nursing. I have always seen myself as a caring and conscientious person and hoped this career would enable me to ultimately join David in New Zealand.

Mrs Maloney still treated me as a convenient unpaid babysitter and I felt in need of escaping the rather stifling home life there. Now twenty years old, I found a bed sitting room with the Roche family in Harvey

Road, Guildford, a short walk up the hill from St Luke's hospital where I applied to do my three year State Registration training. Matron Bridget Coyle (Biddy) interviewed me and was most disconcerted at my refusal to live in the Nurses' Home.

"It is good for girls to have the companionship and the discipline," she insisted.

I remained adamant.

"I have had eleven years at boarding schools and have accommodation not far away," I replied.

Eventually she capitulated. The next preliminary training school did not start for a couple of months so I was employed as an assistant on the isolation ward.

My experiences there remain some of the most vivid of my brief nursing career. The ward consisted of separate rooms off a long corridor. Centrally were the kitchen, Sister's office, sluice room and other essential areas. The Sister in charge, Sister Watkins, was middle-aged, very petite with her hair neatly in a bun. She peered over her pebble lens spectacles and warmly encouraged me for performing whatever small task she had set me.

"Nurse Barnston, you have set out the patient's lunch tray beautifully."

Whilst there, I had the doubtful privilege of witnessing some diseases that nowadays are rarely seen. Little Roland, only seven years old, was admitted with suspected diphtheria. His very blond hair and pallid face belied his high fever. His dreadful brassy cough and his constant crying in pain distressed me. Masks were always worn when treating patients on the isolation ward. Sister called me over to look at his throat which was covered by evil, ugly, white leathery looking patches. Once the throat swabs proved positive, Roland was promptly transferred to the Isolation Hospital. He was the only child of titled parents who had considered immunisation unnecessary. I did hear later that he survived.

It made a great impression on me, so my family and I have always kept up to date with inoculations to protect us against these preventable diseases.

Tetanus still has the same fifty per cent chance of survival as in those days, if you are unlucky enough to contract it. Reggie, a ginger-haired, freckle-faced young man in his twenties, was too ill to be moved and we were warned to avoid making sudden noises, as these could cause him to go into a spasm. These spasms were extremely distressing to witness. They must have been even more terrifying to experience. His head arched backwards, his hands and jaw clenched (hence the popular name "lockjaw"), his body went quite rigid, so that he was resting on his heels. I believe the treatment was and is curare. This was traditionally used by the South American Indians to paralyse their victims. Reggie spent weeks heavily sedated, with his muscles paralysed, but he did make a slow recovery.

Tuberculosis, alas, is still very much a reality. In those days it was a common malady — particularly pulmonary T.B. or, as it was more commonly called, consumption. Four individual chalets formed part of the isolation ward specifically for nursing these patients. Fresh air was considered essential to recovery, so one side was open to the elements. Only one was occupied whilst I was there. Paddy McCann, an elderly Irishman with a very uncertain temper, sat propped up on his pillows. He yelled, "Nurse, oi want me teeth put in and oi can't reach 'em!" or "Oi'm not going ter drink any more o' this filthy mook!"

Referring to the foul-tasting medicine known as P.A.S. Sister once asked me to taste it so that I could appreciate just how vile it was. By far the most repulsive task I remember in my brief nursing career, was measuring and disposing of his blood-stained sputum. Ugh!

In contrast, the incident when Mrs Murphy was transferred from the maternity ward caused many giggles among the nursing staff. Derek, Mrs Murphy's eldest child, had been at the Nursery School I had recently resigned from. He had contracted measles and it was feared she might have been incubating this very infectious disease (in fact she did not contract it). She was delighted to see a familiar face in this alien environment. The maternity nurses did not constantly wear masks as we had to. The delivery of her fourth child had been straightforward, her baby daughter a healthy addition to their happy family. The local Roman Catholic priest, Father Tom Sheehy was a great friend of the Maloney family with whom I had lived for many years and frequently joined them for a meal. Afterwards I made a cup of tea for us all and it was often too weak for him.

"Call this tea, Eve?" he exclaimed, "more like horse's pee"!

Many times he called and said "How about some 'horse's', Eve?"

He visited the patients regularly. Mrs Murphy was one of his parishioners. To Sister's surprise Father greeted me warmly and demanded some "horse's". You can imagine quite a bit of explanation was needed to remove the look of consternation from poor Sister Watkins' face. I made the tea and found some milk in a tall glass jug in the fridge. He sat in Sister's office chatting and enjoying his tea, then bade us farewell. A short while later Nurse Jones went to the fridge to collect the expressed breast milk for the baby and found the jug nearly empty. Poor Nurse Jones was chastised for not labelling it. Fortunately there was plenty more milk where that came from! Sister consoled me when I reproached myself saying, "Don't worry dear, Father never suspected a thing and it was good Catholic milk!"

CHAPTER
FIVE

I studied in the P.T.S. Exams were such a worry
On "Gynaecology" I learned to "hurry, hurry, hurry."

In February at the age of twenty I commenced my training by spending three months concentrated study under Sister Tutor's stern eye. Her hair never varied. Neat sausage curls drawn back from her very high forehead made us wonder if it was detachable!

Ten students, two men and eight women, from a variety of nationalities and backgrounds were given our uniforms. The men wore white coats. We wore blue and white striped dresses with a white apron. A square of starched linen was formed into a cap and pleated into a "tail". These we learned to model over our knee to get the correct shape, until we soon became proficient. Our rather dramatic looking navy blue, scarlet lined cloaks protected us from the elements.

Once we passed our first year State Preliminary Exam and were no longer classed as probationers, our caps changed to a small neat one, much easier to manipulate. Our white belts signified nothing. Staff Nurses wore a navy belt with an ornate silver buckle. My ambition was to achieve this lofty status. The Ward

Sisters dressed in navy blue with plain caps, Matron's cap was frilled. She was a formidable woman much held in awe.

I enjoyed my P.T.S. The practical lectures consisted of bed making, setting up trays or trolleys for various procedures such as mouth cleaning, catheterisation, giving an enema.

We were taught to apply leeches by washing the area thoroughly and moistening it with milk. The part to be leeched was then covered with dry lint containing a hole to be placed over the desired area. The leech was held in a towel and applied. Sugar and water were used on the site if it was reluctant to suck. It is only one and a half inches long but can expand to six inches when gorged with blood. Then it drops off spontaneously. If it does not, it can be released by sprinkling salt on it, NEVER pull it. (Thank God, I never had to put this archaic theory into practice.)

The leeches are a source of hirudin, a powerful anti-coagulant secreted by their buccal glands that also anaesthetises the area to which it is applied. I have heard that in certain cases they are still being used.

The poet Wordsworth said of the leech gatherer —

> "He told that to these waters he had come
> To gather leeches, being old and poor:
> Employment hazardous and wearisome!"

Rubbing backs was an essential routine, as in those days, patients remained bed bound for considerable time. The modern approach of "out of bed" the day after the operation was unthinkable.

"A pressure sore is a sign of poor nursing." Sister Tutor repeated this fact emphatically. I can still remember the mnemonic for memorising the causes — "Pray For Me" P.F.M.: Pressure, Friction, Moisture, and the one for the type of patient most vulnerable — "HIP TOE": Helpless, Incontinent, Paralysed, Toxaemic, Oedematous, Emaciated.

Other mnemonics are "A Red Indian though he might eat toffee in church" for the spelling of ARITHMETIC and "Elephants in straw hats" to remember the "dot" letters in Morse Code and "Take more Ovaltine" for the "dashes". "Richard of York gained battles in vain" reminds me of the colours of the rainbow — red, orange, yellow, green, blue, indigo, violet.

Some useless information stays embedded in the brain forever. Nick's father's Rolls Royce number was YT 1131. Recently on a television programme I saw a similar model Rolls Royce, number "YT" but not 1131. It revived many memories.

Another incident concerns magpies. When I came to Australia and heard magpies warbling every day, it reminded me of the stories I was told when young. It is unlucky because it was the only bird which refused to enter the Ark, preferring to perch on the roof. A little rhyme we had covering magpies —

"One means anger, two brings mirth
Three a wedding, four a birth.
Five is heaven, six is hell
But seven's the very Devil's ain sell."

Trivia that has remained with me is where to look for a rainbow when the sun is shining and it is raining at the same time. Stand with your back to the sun and the rainbow is opposite you.

We also had lectures on Anatomy and Physiology about which I knew nothing, as I had studied NO science of any kind whilst at school. I really enjoyed these and painstakingly drew careful diagrams for my notes. Our talks on ethics caused a minor furore when the perennial subject of using animals for experiments was raised. Sister was confronted by Nurse Wilson, a florid faced, big boned girl who vehemently argued this subject. Sister said, "Would you prefer tests to be performed on humans as they have been in concentration camps?"

These atrocities were only too recent and made many of us rethink our objections.

We visited the Water Works and local Sewage Works for our community health projects and also studied elementary dietetics. Bandaging was fun as we practised on each other. Our lectures continued throughout our training on a regular basis. Later these dealt with specific diseases and their treatment, nowadays far more technical and sophisticated. To test a diabetic's level of sugar involved filling a test tube with thirty minims of blue Benedicts solution and adding three minims of urine. This we held over a bunsen burner and boiled for two minutes, recording and noting the exact change of colour indicating the amount of sugar. Sometimes the blue turned to green or to yellow and in some cases orange. Nowadays a minor prick on the thumb and an electronic glucometer gives an immediate and accurate reading.

Once our concentrated three months studying was completed we sat the hospital entrance exam. Not everyone passed, but yes, I came second! We were then allocated to various wards as REAL probationers. I don't know if the wards were named after prominent people, but my first placement was "Sells" for gynaecological patients. This was quite a shock to me with my sheltered upbringing. I knew the theory of how babies were born, but any other conditions such as miscarriages or abortions and hysterectomies were all mysteries. I needed to be a fast learner as there were twenty five beds on the ward, usually all occupied. My duties as the newest probationer were centred on the sluice. I prepared, distributed, emptied and sterilised bedpans. This was a continuous task as we had patients with urinary problems sharing the gynaecological ward.

One tragedy when I had only been on the ward a month, was the admission of Stephanie Roberts. We had been to Tech together. She had failed her N.N.E.B. and was repeating part of the course. I remembered her as an attractive girl with fluffy fair hair and a healthy complexion. Now her face was waxen and she was barely conscious. She had realised she was pregnant and ignorantly tried to abort the baby by inserting a knitting needle. She was haemorrhaging severely and only survived until the next day. This made a huge impact on me, the more so having known her personally.

Each evening all the flowers were removed from the bedside lockers. Each morning my task was to replenish the water and re-arrange them. I loved doing this but rarely had time to indulge any artistic skills. Everything was "hurry, hurry, hurry". I have never been a person who acts particularly speedily and was constantly harassed by Staff Nurse to, "Get a move on Nurse Barnston, we haven't got all day."

I learned to move quickly, quickly!

Sister, a stickler for correctness, checked every tray or trolley prepared by junior nurses.

"Remember," she said, as Nurse Smith prepared the tray for a pessary insertion, "everything that enters the vagina MUST be sterilised."

This famous saying of hers caused suppressed giggles each time.

Mrs Wilkins, a large, genial lady with a face like a distorted potato, had complications with her hysterectomy. Normally patients were kept in bed for two weeks and allowed home at the end of the third. When I arrived she had already been ensconced for some time and knew all the other patients' diagnoses and most of the details of their families.

"Nurse, 'ere a minute, luv," she called.

I hastened to her bedside, hoping she was not haemorrhaging again.

"Be a ducks and ask Mrs Browning if 'er Alfie would get me some of them 'air nets like wot she 'as, when 'e visits?"

Mrs Wilkins had no visitors. A widow, her only child went to Canada during the war and married over there.

"My Shirl," she announced proudly as she fondled the worn photo, "she done orlright for 'erself, 'er Ernie, 'e's a bus driver in Toronto."

Visitors were on Wednesday evenings and Sunday afternoons only. They waited uneasily outside the ward in their best clothes, laden with flowers and grapes and carrier bags. Only two at a time were allowed and children never. They stood at the door anxiously searching the beds with their eyes until they spied their mothers. Frantic waving, blowing of kisses and hand signals ensued.

Duty hours at the hospital were long. There were only two shifts. The day staff started at eight a.m. and finished at eight p.m. Two hours were allowed off during the day. We had either ten until twelve off, two until four or prior to our precious day off, we finished at six. The night staff were on duty from eight until eight. This made it a long night with only an hour's break for a meal but was compensated for by having TWO days off a week.

The house where I had my bed sitting room, a short walk up the hill from the hospital, had no bathroom. Mrs Roche bathed the two small children in a portable zinc bath that hung on a hook outside the kitchen. She and her husband had their weekly bath at her mother's home nearby. I took my towel and soap to the Public Baths, a grim red brick building adjacent to the Swimming Baths. Here for a shilling, I could wallow as long as I liked in a cubicle containing a deep bath. I soon thought of a way to save my precious shilling.

I would sneak into the Nurses' Home with my friend June when Home Sister wasn't around and have a bath there. Usually I made it a quick one as I lived in constant fear of being caught. Looking back on it now, I doubt if the authorities would have had any objections to a nurse being hygienically conscientious!

Nick had been stationed in the North of England and although still friendly, our paths had diverged. Tony Newman was my new boyfriend. His name was actually Michael Anthony Newman, what initials! He lived with his parents and sister Pat in Stoughton, a suburb of Guildford. I had no idea what he did at the Royal Aircraft Establishment at Farnborough as he had taken the "Official Secrets Act" oath and never divulged a thing. He was tall with fair straight hair and an infectious smile. His family were very kind and having lacked a family life of my own, I appreciated their warmth. A keen Sea Scout, he introduced me to the movement and his colleagues where they met by the river at Shalford in the Scout hut. I later started a Cub group there with the help of Mickey and Derek.

I remember Pat wearing a rather low cut frock when her French pen-friend stayed with them, and his remark, "Oh Pat, zat dress makes me zink bad zinks!"

Tony had a motor bike and I just loved riding pillion and feeling the wind in my hair — no helmets then. Sometimes at weekends we would spend the day at the coast, Bognor or Brighton were favourites. The weather was often windy and wet but it didn't detract from the adventure of a day away. We saved hard and managed to have a wonderful week's holiday near

Torquay. We explored the beautiful Devon countryside and stopped for tea at quaint little roadside tea rooms. The weather was perfect. In those days we didn't dream of sharing a bedroom, it was strictly separate rooms. We HEARD of couples booking in at notorious venues such as Brighton as "Mr and Mrs Smith", but would never have done so ourselves. Our Scout/Guide background plus religious convictions affected our moral decisions.

CHAPTER
SIX

Bedpans and "bottles", working through the night,
Visiting the mortuary and getting such a fright.

After my spell in "Sells" I had my first taste of night duty. "Poyle" the men's medical ward saw me as the respectful very junior nurse on duty with Nurse Sims. She only had a few months to go before State Registration. Short and stocky, she alternated between trying to study during our quiet moments or snapping orders when some crisis occurred. She had recently become engaged, a surprise to many of us as she was one of the older nurses. She must have been in her early thirties, which to me then seemed positively ancient. Her favourite song which she hummed snatches of was apt and very popular at the time — Frank Sinatra's "Young at Heart".

"Fairy tales can come true, it can happen to you
If you're young at heart.
And it's hard you will find, to be narrow of mind
If you're young at heart.
You can go to extremes, with impossible schemes,

You may laugh when your dreams fall apart at
   the seams
But life gets more exciting every passing day
And love is either in your heart or on its way . . ."

Night duty was hard to adjust to, especially "living
out". The Roche household with two young children
was not a quiet place and on my two days off, it wasn't
until the second day that I felt relatively human. It was
rare that I enjoyed a Saturday night off either on night
or day duty, but when I did, Tony and I went to the
dance at the Drill Hall. Guildford boasted an Army
Barracks and many of the soldiers attended these
weekly hops. I heard Johnny Dankworth and his
famous wife Cleo Laine at the beginning of their
career. Although I have always had a good sense of
rhythm I never learned to dance, something I have
always regretted. Tony had "two left feet" so we went
mainly as an enjoyable social outing. A couple of
instances stand out in my memory during my months
on night duty.

   The first death I had to deal with was a Mr Day who
had died of testicular cancer. Nurse Sims and I went
through the complicated ritual of laying him out. Part
of this procedure included cutting the corpse's finger
and toe nails. Ever since, this is a task I have abhorred.
Something Nurse Sims said has always remained
potently with me.

   "This isn't Mr Day anymore," she said, "it is only his
shell and a shell is something that is disposable."

There was a dear man called Mr Andrews who was not very old, but each evening as I came on duty he seemed to be fading a little more. One evening when Nurse Sims was having her meal I was left alone, in charge of the ward of sleeping men. As I walked through checking them, I saw Mr Andrews' face was a waxy white, his lips were blue and his jaw hung open and his stertorous breathing had stopped. Anxiously I took his pulse, nothing at all, he wasn't breathing. Panic! As I had been instructed by Nurse, "In an emergency, phone Night Sister". This is what I did.

"Mr Andrews is d'd'd'dead," I stammered.

"What?" she screamed down the phone, "I'm coming right now, and don't EVER let me hear you make such a remark again. Only a doctor or qualified nurse can diagnose death."

She came straight away. I had already had my meal so when Nurse Sims returned we laid him out. I accompanied him to the mortuary, a small building in the grounds. The night was velvety black and as the trolley was wheeled across a bumpy path, Mr Andrews' knees shot up. No pun intended, but I nearly died of fright! The kindly mortician had to sit me in his office and revive me with a cup of tea.

Each evening I chanted the nightly refrain as I went to prepare the patients' drinks — "Tea, coffee, cocoa, Ovaltine or Bovril?"

Many were on strict diets that had to be adhered to. Mr Browning, a diabetic, who was in to have his insulin level controlled, would try to cadge sweets from the other patients or demand tea with two sugars hoping the new probationer would know no better.

The nights seemed very long. About three a.m. was often the time patients died, at this hour MY energy level plummeted too

Night Sister did her round with a huge torch which often woke the lighter sleepers. One of my jobs was to make cups of tea for the wakeful patients. Then I took doses of "Pot Brom and Chloral" to those who didn't sleep or caused a disturbance. Sister's office boasted a small electric heater and on quiet nights once the patients were settled, I was sometimes allowed into this sanctum with Nurse Sims, and I too attempted to study.

We woke the patients early as many procedures had to be completed before the day staff took over. We took bowls of warm water to each bed-ridden patient. Many needed help with the morning wash and shave. We distributed the medications, filled the water jugs with fresh water, made the beds and if necessary changed them, took the breakfasts to each patient and cleared away, then of course the eternal bedpan and "bottle" rounds.

The pink overalled ward maid came on duty very early, sweeping and polishing and livening up the morning with her cheerful chatter.

"An' 'ow are you this mornin' ducks?" she asked each patient. At last, at a quarter to eight Nurse Sims handed over her report to the Sister of the ward. I exchanged a few pleasantries with Nurse Byron Bethune, my replacement, then off to supper and bed. I was not sorry when my stretch of night duty came to an end and I was given one week's holiday.

The first few days I spent just recovering but then I took a couple of my regular train trips to London. Aunty Toppie, my father's cousin, and her husband Uncle Vivian owned a wholesale woollens business just off Regent Street in the West End. She was the epitome of elegance and my main source of clothing! I willingly accepted her highly unsuitable, middle-aged dresses as new ones were NOT on my list of priorities. My brown overcoat from school days lasted me for years and years. (Whilst on duty, nurses wore red woollen lined navy blue cloaks for warmth and for protection against the elements.) I usually shared Uncle Vivian's lunch which invariably consisted of smoked salmon sandwiches, a delicacy I still enjoy.

Then I happily window shopped along Oxford Street and turned into Manchester Square for my "pilgrimage" to the Wallace Collection. As a child I lived for a time just around the corner. The magnificent collection of paintings included Frans Hals' famous "Laughing Cavalier". The charming pastoral scenes and portraits by Fragonard and Boucher delighted me as much as ever. Then, if it was summer time when the evenings were light until ten o'clock, I caught the bus to Cricklewood to visit dear Auntie Ella. She was my mother's "double" cousin and had been her very close friend. I describe her as "double" because my grandfather was one of twin brothers who between them married three sisters causing all relations to be DOUBLY related.

After Aunt Toppie's often derogatory and astringent remarks it was a relief to visit Aunt Ella. Not only had she been my mother's cousin but also her best friend. A short lady with "pebble" glasses and matronly figure, she was warm, caring and genuine. Her small, well stocked garden was her pride as was her prolific greenhouse. I came away laden with freshly picked fruit and vegetables and often a few tins of luxury items too. She really spoiled me and I loved it! She and Uncle Harry were the only relations I could relate to. My father, a very mild, introverted man had become quite withdrawn after my mother's untimely death when I was just eleven. I never lived with him after that sad event and considered him as a kindly, rather remote figure, albeit with a good and subtle sense of humour.

Now dear Uncle Harry was totally different. He loved to remind me that for his third birthday all he wanted was a baby sister. My mother actually arrived on the day and he regarded her as his special mascot. Many adjectives could be used to describe him, eccentric, charming, outrageous, unconventional and unbelievable! Most of all he was understanding and loving towards me. One of my friends said, "Everyone loves your Uncle Harry, he is 'larger than life' and the roguish twinkle in his eye is irresistible."

It certainly was, for he attracted women until he was well into his eighties. Pre World War I, amongst other things, he imported cars from the Continent for the "idle rich". Later he went into business with, and was the great friend of Raymond Way, the millionaire motor magnate. He had extensive interests in the motor trade.

Uncle Harry's life had been very adventurous but he appreciated his freedom and never married. Many a time I would stay overnight with him in his bed-sitting room in London's West End. Sometimes I had the bed, sometimes the couch. The though of any impropriety never crossed my mind and I doubt it did his. He indulged my healthy appetite and delighted in taking me to the many famous restaurants where he was well known. Before my mother died, he had assured her that he would look after David and me. My eldest brother Jack had died in 1941 so there were just the two of us. He kept his word and even visited David and family in New Zealand. As for me, he was always caring and available. I loved him dearly.

The other person I visited in London was my school friend Maureen. She was a librarian at the famous Art Library in the Victoria and Albert Museum. The incredible treasures housed there never failed to enthral me. For many years I would meet her in the Museum Restaurant for lunch and exchange news. She and her husband Paddy have remained dear and faithful friends.

CHAPTER
SEVEN

Nursing on the Medical ward, the Children's, "Skins" and "Eyes,"
King George's death. I sat exams and even won a prize.

Returning to the hospital after my welcome break
I wondered what new experience was in store for me.
I was transferred to "Astolat", the women's Medical
ward. This also included a side ward that specialised
in Dermatology. Here we nursed some of the appalling
cases of eczema and psoriasis. Powerful ointments
were carefully applied to specific lesions. As these
contained strong acid, we had the danger impressed
upon us. I was always glad to be a junior nurse who
only assisted at these painful sessions.

The small ophthalmic ward was also part of the
medical ward. The patients here had operations that
involved them being absolutely immobilised.
Sandbags each side of the head kept them quite still.
Mrs Nash had a detached retina and had been in the
ward some weeks, not allowed to do a thing for herself.
Her husband served in the Navy. Her children were
quite young and needed temporary care in a residential
home. The poor lady worried and fretted but had to
be kept totally immobile for six weeks. Another

patient, Mrs Stuart, was terrified. "Will I be blind?" she wailed after her straightforward cataract operation. She was nursed sitting up and both eyes were kept bandaged for three days, very frightening. It was with a great sense of relief when the bandages were removed that her "good" eye was as good as ever. Although she hated receiving the regular eye drops that were necessary, and made a terrible fuss, her sight improved daily.

We had many different conditions to nurse on the general medical ward. Mrs Smith, a sweet refined lady who insisted on putting her hair in curlers each evening, was suffering from syphilis and receiving mercury treatment. Sister explained the syphilis had affected her general nervous system and she would end up in the infirmary at the local Asylum as she would develop G.P.I. (General Paralysis of the Insane). The horror of this has always remained with me. We had numerous heart patients, stomach conditions, diabetics in to be stabilised and one case that I remember vividly.

A middle aged lady was admitted with leukaemia. She was desperately ill and a pathetic sight. I realised with shock that I knew Mrs Gray. Some years earlier during the war I had boarded with her and her spoilt daughter Ann in Farnham. She had been very unkind to me and now I had her at my mercy. This poor woman had only a few more weeks to live. Revenge is certainly not in my nature. I remembered Ann as a podgy, spoilt disagreeable little girl. What a surprise when this pleasant, tall, attractive young lady came to visit her mother. She told me of her father's death, his ship had been torpedoed. She still lived in the same home.

My nickname whilst at St Luke's was "Nurse Arrowroot." The reason for this was my slight speech defect and inability to pronounce the letter "R" correctly. When I went to make up some arrowroot for a patient, I announced, "Here you are Mrs Jones, here's your 'awowoot'!"

A couple of events took place whilst I was on this ward. My twenty first birthday would have been a total non-event as I was on duty as usual, so I decided I ought to have a cake. I went to Fullers tea shop in the High Street and bought one of their distinctive walnut layer cakes. Delicious American icing covered this luxury. I naïvely took it to the ward and gave each patient a morsel. What chastisement I received from strict Sister Buller! (Her nickname was "Bully" for good reason.) Many of the women were on strict diets such as the gastric and diabetic patients. I felt deep pangs of guilt for years afterwards. In retrospect, I doubt if the small quantity they ate would have harmed them. To my great surprise they had very kindly clubbed together and bought me a bookshelf that can fold flat. I have always treasured it. I still have it and the accompanying card. When I see the signatures, I can visualise many of the faces AND their illnesses. Tony gave me a gold cross and chain. Dad had forgotten but bought me a lovely pair of gloves when reminded!

The other event was the annual Prizegiving day. Another surprise for me! I was to receive the award for Theoretical and Practical Nursing for my year. What a kerfuffle! I was given a new apron and cap for the event. I practised walking up to receive my prize, and received instructions to make sure my shoes were shining, there were no ladders in my black stockings and no wisps of elusive hair escaping my cap.

This very formal occasion totally intimidated me, but I felt so amazed to receive this unexpected prize that secretly I was delighted. The book, published in Australia, was entitled "Surgical Nursing" by H. C. Rutherford Darling and T. Edward Wilson. I remember my surprise on reading that catgut used for sutures was really sheepgut. This needed complicated disinfecting to destroy the bacteria. Kangaroo tendon was NOT the natural habitat of bacteria. It explains in great detail how to remove the tendon from the synovial sheath of the animal's tail and how it needs to be stored in a glass stoppered jar in 0.4 percent Binoidide of Mercury solution — and these facts were presented to me twenty years before I thought of immigrating to Australia! The book awarded me at the presentation is something I still treasure.

After my brief moment of glory it was back to the ward and the rounds of asking the patients, "Have you BEEN?", checking on the state of their bowels. If the answer was "no", we reported to Staff Nurse who ordered an aperient suitable for the patient's condition.

Each morning, at a pre-arranged time, Matron made her rounds. She demanded perfection. The bedside lockers were hastily tidied and adjusted to the correct angle. The bed trolleys had to be exactly parallel to each other at the foot of each bed and the patients lay neatly "at attention"! All corners on the sheets and white counterpanes were geometrically symmetrical, and the pillowcases openings AWAY from the doors. I have no idea for the reason for this particular quirk, but I adhere to it to this day.

The other awe inspiring event was when a Consultant made his weekly visit. Sister always kowtowed to these physicians. We juniors kept a respectful distance from these impressive deities, usually busying ourselves in the sluice. Once I was summoned when the dermatologist made his rounds. I felt dumbfounded when ushered into his presence. To my surprise, Sister who usually snarled commands at me, actually smiled!

"Mr Boxall wants to know how young Angela Parker is responding to her new treatment?" Staff Nurse was at lunch and it was the senior nurse's day off. I was relieved to discover that this hallowed being was an ordinary man after all. I explained Angela's progress to the best of my ability and felt ten feet tall!

After my time on the medical ward my next move was to "Harper" the children's ward. Sister Brown did NOT like any N.N.E.B. qualified student nurses. She made this clear to me from the beginning.

"Don't think you know everything just because you can change a nappy or prepare the feeds," she admonished. In retrospect she should have appreciated and utilised what knowledge I already had.

I did NOT enjoy my time on the ward although I dearly loved children. When they were seriously ill as many were, it upset me greatly and when they were not too ill, they took some controlling. This was the case with a lively young patient called Henry. He was about six, old enough to know better. He had inadvertently swallowed an open brooch which could have been very dangerous causing peritonitis had it pierced him internally. The poor boy had restricted fluids and was given cotton wool sandwiches to eat. I pleaded with Sister and she allowed him a smear of jam to make them slightly more palatable. As junior nurse it was my unenviable task to check everything he passed, searching for the offending brooch. On the third day I was successful and he was discharged with a stern warning. I discovered the offending brooch was a Women's Institute badge with the motto emblazoned on it "For Home and Country". I muttered to Nurse Sims, "The things I do for home and country!"

Annette, who suffered from a form of anaemia, was admitted for her regular blood transfusion. She not only took her first steps but also had her first birthday on the ward. When a child was unlucky enough to have a birthday in hospital, there was always a cake and by an unspoken tradition, Sister danced for us all as we sang —

"Knees up, Sister Brown, knees up, Sister Brown,
Under the table you must go, ee eye ee eye ee eye oh
And if I catch you bending, I'll chop your knees right off,

Knees up, knees up, don't get the breeze up —
    knees up, Sister Brown!"

One dear little boy, the only child of older parents was seriously ill with a type of nephritis. Ian HAD to drink milk. We tried flavouring it, colouring it and used other disguises. He had a craze on "Nurse Arnson" as he called me, he couldn't say "Barnston". Many a time my off duty hours were used trying to persuade him to consume this essential drink.

Only one child died whilst I nursed on this ward. Sister had a strict rule that only she and Staff Nurse laid out the little body, never a student nurse. Very humane — (thank God).

Christmas was a very special time in the hospital. Having no family of my own to go to, I was only too pleased to spend the day on duty. All children well enough went home but sadly many very sick ones remained on the ward. Father Christmas visited in the morning and gave each child a well chosen gift. We decorated the ceilings with paper chains and a good sized fir tree stood outside Sister's office with colourful baubles and tarnished tinsel. This was in the days before foil tinsel was available and the silver tinsel acquired a dull golden sheen. At lunch time, with due pomp and ceremony, the surgeon arrived, donned his chef's hat and carved the turkey to obsequious applause. We all laughed at his weak jokes.

Then the time came for us to take our Preliminary State Examination in February 1952. The venue was the prestigious St George's Hospital at Hyde Park

Corner in London. We travelled by train and bus dressed in our freshly starched uniforms and scarlet lined cloaks. I had studied extra hard the previous weeks and found to my relief that the questions were not too hard. It happened to be one of the days just after King George VI had died and he was Lying in State in Westminster Hall for the three days prior to his funeral.

"Let's go," said Jill, one of my colleagues.

"All right," I agreed, "but I'm sure there will be a long queue."

As soon as the officials saw us in our uniform they ushered us ahead of every one else, presuming we had come during our off duty time!

The four foot high catafalque on which the coffin was placed was proudly guarded by four of the Household troop in their plumed helmets and four colourful Yeomen of the Guard.

"Who are those other two men?" whispered Jill.

"I don't know, but we'll find out," I said.

They were the King's Gentlemen at Arms in their full uniform. I later heard that the queues were up to three miles long and over three hundred thousand respectful subjects filed past the catafalque to mourn their beloved monarch. It was an awe-inspiring, never to be forgotten sight.

CHAPTER
EIGHT

To the County hospital I had to be transferred
For Orthopaedic training. Then exciting news I heard.

St Luke's Hospital had no orthopaedic department, this was housed at the Royal Surrey County Hospital the other side of Guildford. This was to be my next ward. This lovely old town has a steep cobbled High Street, the River Wey runs in the valley and opposite the North Downs rise to another steep hill. It was a long bike ride to get to my new post so I decided to leave Harvey Road and board with one of the nurses.

Nurse Elizabeth Isard had recently married and was buying a house not far from the County Hospital in Denzil Road. Here I had the luxury of two rooms. One was my bed-sitting room, the other small one I made into a kitchen. I had a "Wee Baby Belling" electric stove and a bowl for my washing up and washing. The lavatory was down the steep stairs and outside around the back of the house, a long trek. Here also was a tap where I filled my large jug. I clumsily tumbled on the stairs with it initially. Hastily I mopped up the puddles before anyone arrived home.

After that I carried water very gingerly up to my room. I revelled in this luxury after only one room. I had a bed, a small table and chair where I ate and studied and a small curtained corner where I hung my clothes. There was no chest of drawers so my other few possessions resided in my faithful suitcase.

The men's orthopaedic ward, "Jarvis", was a very new experience for me. Many of the young men were motor bike accidents. Guildford was between London and Portsmouth where there was a large Naval Base. Two of the cases of fractured femurs were young, very lively sailors, David and Jamie. They loved teasing us young nurses and we enjoyed having such handsome, cheerful young lads to care for. We also had cases of deformities being corrected as in the case of young Edmund. He was the darling of the ward, a blue eyed, curly haired boy of about fifteen. He had endured numerous operations on his spine and apparently was referred to as "our regular customer"!

Another spinal case was Mark. He had been sent from Newcastle in the very north of England to be operated on by Mr Golden the prestigious orthopaedic surgeon. (His Registrar was Mr Baikie for whom we all swooned.) Mark had a tumour removed from his spine and was nursed completely flat, all he could move were his arms and as Nurse Bates warned me, "Watch out if you get within range of those enthusiastic arms!"

Mark seemed quite middle aged to me with his thinning sandy hair and fund of wartime experiences, although his records showed he was thirty two. He had no visitors and was single. His mother wrote regularly and during my off duty I would often write and send a dictated letter back to her. I also did minor shopping for him. He became very attached to me and I still have a letter he wrote to me when he was recovering. Poor Mark, I wonder what became of him.

A friend of mine, a very tall nurse called Beryl, told me this story years later. One of her similarly totally bedridden patients she found very attractive and apparently the feeling was reciprocated. She was about six feet tall and dreaded having a shorter husband, so one night while he slept, she got the tape measure out and discovered he was about three inches taller than her. All was well, the romance flourished, they married and had two delightful, very tall daughters.

When I was born, my mother proudly showed me off to her sister who duly admired the new baby, but remarked, "What lumpy hips she has!" Unfortunately I was not only cursed with big hips, but my right one would click in and out of the socket, a condition known not surprisingly as "clicking hip". As a schoolgirl my "party trick" was to let my friends feel it as it clicked dramatically in and out.

Nursing involved a lot of heavy work and the continual lifting had aggravated the condition and caused a severe case of bursitis. I was not only in considerable pain with my right hip, but occasionally it would just lock, to my acute embarrassment. My doctor referred me to the orthopaedic surgeon who decided an operation was necessary to remove the lesser trochanter — part of the femur. I had already had the privilege of seeing an artificial hip joint installed in one of our patients. They were referred to as an "acrylic head", for that is what they used to form the new joint. In those days that particular operation was in its infancy and was not always the success that it usually is today. Before any date could be decided upon for my operation, I had a very exciting compulsory week's holiday. This was reluctantly awarded me by Matron, insisted upon by no other than the Mayor of Guildford himself.

CHAPTER
NINE

What an honour! Maid of Honour to the Festival Queen.
A busy and dramatic week. No hospital routine.

England had suffered from austerity for some years
after the end of World War II. Now with great
economic growth and technological advances,
unemployment had decreased and a degree of material
affluence ushered in a period of booming economy.

To rejoice in this new prosperity, in 1951 the
Festival of Britain continued to be celebrated around
the country for a year. The Festival Hall and the huge
Fun Fair in Battersea Park were two of the many
permanent monuments. MINE was a string of pearls
given to me by the Mayor of Guildford as a memento.

Guildford decided on a Festival week in July 1952.
In May, they started the selection of a Festival Queen.
To my surprise Tony had put forward my name. This
was definitely not a beauty contest, no swimsuit
parade! We were interviewed and questioned by
a panel of judges. I remember wearing a very plain
purple shirtwaister dress with self smocking on the
skirt. In those days apart from having hefty hips the
rest of me was slim. Imagine my embarrassment when

I saw that one of the judges was the then famous David Dunhill, our old youth club leader. He told me afterwards that he'd have liked me to win but was concerned about being biased! The next week's newspaper showed a photo of us eight finalists chosen out of the thirty seven who had been in the original group.

When the day for the final selection arrived, I had to swap my off duty to enable me to attend. Now we were questioned in detail as to our ambitions, availability, and background.

"What would the people of Guildford most like to see in their Queen?" was one question. I answered, "Friendliness".

This, along with a long article, was quoted in the newspaper. When I returned to the hospital and the patients read it, it was with great glee that these young men called out, "Nurse, nurse, come here, what do you mean by friendliness?" I said they loved to tease.

Daphne Bannister, a rather serious, flat-chested ballet dancer was wisely chosen as the winner. She definitely had the poise and confidence, having been in show business. I came second and a pleasant, rather buxom, shorthand-typist, Eileen Bird, was chosen as Maid of Honour with me.

Then came the problem. I had no holidays due, how was I going to have a full week off work in the middle of my orthopaedic experience?

"Don't worry," said the kindly Mayor, "I will have a word with Matron."

He explained to her that it was a privilege to have one of her nurses chosen for this special event and in the end she capitulated.

Someone said to me that they thought the choice showed a good variety of careers — dancer, nurse and shorthand-typist. In those days other than working in a shop or teaching, there were not a lot of other choices for girls. Personally, I think we were just chosen alphabetically, Bannister, Barnston and Bird!

First we had to be fitted for our dresses. Daphne's was white and Eileen and I wore a soft shade of buttery yellow. We had headdresses to match, rather like bridesmaids. These dresses were made by Vicki, the mother of Christine, the little seven year old crown bearer. Elaine Thompson and Vicki Barter were our official chaperones for the whole week.

My father was NOT pleased about any of this, in fact I think he was acutely embarrassed. Maybe he thought I HAD paraded in a bathing costume! He went away and stayed with his sister in Eastbourne for the week, so the complimentary tickets for the Grand Parade I gave to his brother, my Uncle Manny.

The grounds of Guildford's ancient castle built in the eleventh century were to be the venue for the crowning of the Festival Queen. These gardens have always been nurtured lovingly by the Council and that July was no exception. To quote a newspaper cutting, "No more fitting place could be found for such an occasion. The Castle Keep, with all its historic background, and the gardens ablaze with flowers, is a setting which adds dignity and beauty to the Crowning Ceremony."

The following week, the 4th-12th July 1952 was one of the busiest and most exciting of my life. Each morning a car arrived to collect me at ten o'clock, then I was "on duty" until late each evening.

We attended the Grand Championship Swimming Festival and water polo match at the local Lido (swimming pool). There was a Grand Garden Fête with children's sports events and fancy dress parade. Mothers had gone to a lot of trouble and initiative to produce colourful and original costumes. We watched dancing displays and the adults tug-of-war contest. The ankle contest consisted of a number of hopeful ladies hidden behind a large screen with only their ankles exposed. I remember the winner stammering, "Goodness, not ME, have I REALLY won it?"

She was a tall, gangly teenager with a spotty face and dark hair that stood up like a brush, but obviously she possessed superb ankles.

The Festival Flower Show was a joy; but alas we did not have time to really appreciate the details of this colourful exhibition. We were only there to present the prizes. Daphne's confidence proved her excellent at short improvised speeches.

On the Sunday we had the morning free, but in the afternoon, again in the Castle grounds, was a Service of Dedication by the Provost of Guildford. This was followed by a splendid concert. For the whole week there was a Fire exhibition and demonstration. A photograph of the three of us on a Fire Engine on the Guildford By-Pass actually appeared in the National Press. In the sports area, we watched and applauded the finals of the local cricket matches, the lawn tennis tournaments, the local Cycle Speedway, Greyhound track, Darts Championships, the Festival Bowls tournament, the Athletics match and even the Snooker Club finals.

Each evening there was a dance culminating in the Carnival Ball, a very grand affair. Partners were provided for us by our chaperones. Eileen's boyfriend and Tony were left watching us on the sidelines!

Two rather awe inspiring events for me during that week were the "royal" visits to the local hospitals. Matron "Biddy" of St Luke's entertained us to tea in her office. The Mayor had accompanied us and to my surprise she was toadying to him. It was an amazing experience to visit the wards and appreciate the rigid protocol that was intrinsic to Matron's rounds from the OTHER side.

Similarly Matron at the Royal Surrey County Hospital gave a formal speech of welcome to us and said "I am gratified that one of our nurses is represented in the 'royal party'". I could hardly believe my ears! When she was approached initially to give me special leave for the week, she was quite adamant that one of HER nurses was not going to demean herself in public. It is amazing what power a persuasive Mayor must wield.

When we entered Jarvis ward after our tea and cakes in the sanctum of the Sisters' dining room, the din was horrendous. All the men had acquired the metal bedpans, "bottles" and any other implements they could find to clash together.

"Hip Hip Hooray for Nurse Barnston," they shouted in unison.

Everyone was amused except Matron whose face had turned dark beetroot in anger. "Sister," she commanded, "can you not discipline these patients?"

The kindly Mayor intervened, "they're just showing their appreciation of Nurse Barnston, it's their youthful spirits," he excused them.

They were quite a sight, legs strung up in traction with colourful streamers dangling for the occasion, and a big banner "Hooray for Nurse Barnston" strung across the ward. My face nearly matched Matron's, but from embarrassment and delight, not anger.

I really loved the Baby Show and was delighted that the winner met with my total approval. Judging such a show must be a very difficult task.

Wednesday was early closing day in Guildford. Shops opened all day on Saturday and some towns had Wednesday and some Thursday when they closed at midday. This evening we revelled in the Grand Carnival Procession. There were categories for everyone. Individuals in fancy dress, bicycles, motor bikes, horses, cars and lots of floats for commercial organisations and many of the clubs that abounded in the district. We were driven in a vintage car and were taught how to wave regally at the excited crowds who lined the streets. I am afraid my hand's genteel flutter turned into an enthusiastic acknowledgment when I saw someone I knew.

"Look, look, there's Nurse Barnston," one of my recently recovered patients from the children's ward was held aloft by his father so that he could see me.

Later open air dancing on the Mansion House lawns was followed by a delightful band concert. It was a great pity my father had fled to Eastbourne as he dearly loved brass bands. Still, I expect he walked to the Front there and enjoyed the music at the local Bandstand. We had visited the Fun Fair at Stoke Park earlier in the day, so when I was finally driven home some time after midnight, I fell into bed exhausted.

On the final Saturday, the best day of that unforgettable week, we did not have to start until midday. After lunch we watched the final cricket match on the sports ground, then off to the Cattle Markets for the Children's Pet Show.

"Hello Eve."

One of the mothers from the Nursery School proudly showed me how little Sandra had grown in the intervening years. She was exhibiting her pet rabbit but became very shy when asked to say hello to me. I think all my regalia must have intimidated her.

Then we went down to the river for the Water Gala at St Catherine's. Great pains had been taken over the decorations on our boat. It was a real fun event. One rowing club performed the Swan Lake ballet. Hairy men dressed in tu-tus pranced about and inevitably fell into the water. The Sea Scouts, including Tony, all waved vigorously at me, yelling out and making sure I acknowledged each of them. They performed a skit on gymnastics, again not remaining very dry! The different groups and clubs had gone to immense trouble and initiative decorating their boats. I really don't know how the judges coped, but the prize winning one was modified to resemble that great ship the *Queen Mary*.

We packed such a lot of activities into each day. After opening a school fête that afternoon the Surrey Constabulary gave a display by the police dogs in Stoke Park. This was followed by a military spectacle. The band introduced the various regiments who gave some realistic demonstrations, fortunately only firing blanks. The Square Dancing Club gave a colourful display before we all joined in the final dance of the Festival. Then, to my great delight as a Grand Finale, was a superb fireworks extravaganza. Fireworks have always entranced me. What a week!

CHAPTER
TEN

Feeling sad when Godfrey didn't turn up at the station,
Then I became a patient with my right hip operation.

During the week, Eileen and I became very friendly. She was a straightforward girl with no hang ups. "Queen" Daphne held herself aloof. Unlike Eileen and me, she had no boyfriend and informed us "I'm certainly not jeopardising my career with such frivolities". We both found her a bit of a trial but definitely agreed she was the best choice and we were happy just being ornamental!

It was usual in those days to eat one's main meal in the middle of the day. For the whole week we were fed. (Something I in particular appreciated, usually catering for myself, unlike the other two.) Over the Playhouse cinema was quite a classy restaurant. Here we dined each lunchtime accompanied by our chaperones and the cinema manager James and weedy under manager Godfrey. James was a pock marked, lecherous individual whom we did nothing to encourage. Godfrey was rather shy, and made "sheep's eyes" at us, so Eileen and I developed a plan. We tossed a coin to see which one of us would react to his rather tentative advances. I won. For the rest of the week he showered his attention on ME in particular as I laughed at all his jokes and encouraged his solicitude.

After that eventful week, Godfrey was transferred and became manager of the Plaza cinema, or as it was known locally "the flea-pit". It was by far the most inferior of Guildford's four cinemas as well as being at the "wrong" end of town. Here I visited him and saw many free films. Some of the films I particularly remember there were Spencer Tracy and the beautiful Elizabeth Taylor in "Father of the Bride", "Easter Parade" with Fred Astaire and Judy Garland and the moving film about ballet with Moira Shearer, "The Red Shoes". Going to the pictures was my main form of recreation. I belonged to the local library and still enjoyed an occasional novel when I had time and wasn't studying.

Godfrey took me to a couple of shows in London, a real treat. He had actually managed to get tickets for the stage show of "South Pacific", a never to be forgotten experience. He had arranged to meet me on my day off on the Wednesday so that we could attend the matinée of another new musical but did not turn up at the station. I waited and waited. By this time I realised it was too late for the show and although very disappointed, I was concerned about him. He had always been very reliable but I realised he had no way of contacting me. In those days very few people had a telephone in their house. I knew he boarded over a greengrocer's shop, in a side road, which had a 'phone. When his landlady answered she said, "Poor

Godfrey, he was so worried about abandoning you, but he has just had the doctor in to visit him. He is in bed with severe bronchitis, why don't you call by and see him?"

I walked home for my trusty bike and following the directions she gave me, found Mrs Cooper in her shop. We chatted for a while whilst Godfrey slept. I discovered she had a son Tony, one day younger than "my" Tony and that she and Tony's mother had been in adjacent beds in the maternity ward. Life is full of coincidences. I duly visited Godfrey and went out with him a couple of times before he was transferred to Portsmouth. After that I never saw or heard from him again.

Meanwhile back at the hospital I attended the Annual Ball. Dancing was out of the question. I had managed to conceal my limp fairly well during Festival week, but now my hip was getting more and more painful and the day for my operation loomed. All the nurses swooned over an extremely tall, dark, handsome paratrooper Bill, who had taken out a couple of the Staff Nurses. The Commandos, the "green berets", were the most glamorous army regiments closely followed by the "red berets", the paratroopers.

Imagine my amazement and delight when he spent quite a while that evening chatting to me and actually asked me to go out with him. (Maybe it was my recent fame during Festival week that made him notice me.) I was flattered, flabbergasted and foolish and the envy of all my friends! Poor Tony, I had been going out with him for a couple of years and just suddenly dropped him. How unkind I was. I have often wondered what became of him.

Bill bought me a lovely tennis racquet that I kept until quite recently. We only went out about half a dozen times before his unit was transferred to Scotland. I wrote to him numerous times. He loved peppermint lumps so I saved all my sweet ration and sent him a parcel of them. I never heard from him again. I was devastated, but meanwhile I had my hip operation to cope with.

The Royal Surrey County Hospital had a private ward. Instead of being nursed on a long ward of up to thirty patients, here each person had privacy. As I was a staff member, I was fortunate enough to be a patient there.

Imagine how embarrassing it was for me to be examined by the surgeon, Mr Baikie, whom all we nurses thought was so dishy. It was only a couple of months after Festival week that he operated on my clicking right hip. Something was done to either the greater or lesser trochanter (I forget which) which involved grafting of the gluteus maximus muscle. This graft of the major muscle in my bottom was not immediately successful and unfortunately I was hospitalised much longer than I expected to be. The physiotherapist came daily and amongst other things gave me Faradism treatment involving rhythmical electric shocks whilst I was face down covered only by a sheet.

I remember one morning whilst I was immobilised in this position with my bottom pulsating, I heard a knock on the door.

"Come in" I muttered into the pillow. The door creaked as it opened and then silence. A voice said, "What d'you want ducky, *Telegraph*, *Express* or *Mail*?"

"Oh it's the paper man," I said, "*Daily Telegraph* please."

"I ain't no paper man," was the retort, as he must have gazed amazed at my shrouded, pulsating posterior. "I'm a real flesh and blood man!"

Jarvis ward was immediately below the private ward in this two storey building. I had many letters sent to me from the patients, along with all sorts of unexpected treats. I still treasure a note from Mark and David.

I was kept in hospital for five long weeks when I'd hoped it would be only two. The complications and the fact that I had steep stairs to cope with when I was released (plus no one to look after me), I'm sure delayed my discharge. When I went for my final consultation with Mr Baikie he said, "I'm afraid you will not be able to continue nursing right now, as I don't want you to do any heavy lifting for at least a year. You need to continue weekly physiotherapy sessions for a while, and remember this advice. Never stand when you can sit."

I took his advice and afterwards ALWAYS sat to do my ironing. I bought an adjustable stool that later my children referred to as the "whizzy-round" stool.

I threw aside my crutches before leaving hospital but relied heavily — literally, on my faithful walking stick. I needed this for years, especially when climbing hills. The eleven inch scar on my hip, an ugly red weal, was a constant reminder of my ordeal. I limped for many years.

My promising career was in tatters, rent had to be paid and I also needed to eat, what should I do?

CHAPTER
ELEVEN

Three year olds I taught again when back at Shepherds Hill.
At Mrs Cooper's party I met Don and Win and Will.

When I had been at Shepherds Hill Nursery School,
Diana Mulloy, the mother of a little boy Brian, and I
had become good friends. She told me that Mrs
Cunningham, one of the staff, was pregnant and would
soon be taking six months' leave. She was in charge of
the three year olds which did not demand lifting as
would be the case with the younger children. I applied
for this temporary position and was lucky enough to
get it.

It was a new experience for me having total
responsibility for a group of twenty children. I had an
assistant, Freda, and a student, Shirley. Freda had
been there for many years and remembered me from
the time spent there during my training. She was
extremely competent AND bossy, but I coped happily
enough, allowing her some leeway with the
organisation. I have never felt the need for power!

Most of the children were happy and well adjusted
but we DID have a couple of problems. One extremely
aggressive little boy Leonard bit the other children on

the slightest provocation. The biggest threat was to be sent back to the two year olds' nursery and eventually he realised that his behaviour was unacceptable. The other challenge was Michel, a little French boy who could neither speak nor understand English. It was amazing the speed at which he learned to comprehend and very soon converse as well as the others. He was very musical and loved to sing. We all learned Frère Jacques and then to the same tune using our fingers, sang that perennial children's favourite;

"Where is thumbkin, where is thumbkin?
Here I am, here I am.
How are you this morning?
(wagging thumbs at each other)
Very well I thank you
Run away, run away".

then Peter pointer, tallman, ringman and pinky with the same verse.

Three year olds are at a delightful stage. Usually they are eager to please, toilet trained, getting to be very independent and enjoy playing with others. The twins Stanley and Victor could not have been more different. Stanley was active from the minute he arrived in the morning. He loved climbing outside equipment and was so agile we called him affectionately our little monkey. When the weather was inclement we had sessions of music and movement inside. My not very proficient piano playing was sufficient for the prancing about that used up their excess energy. Victor was considerably quieter, he loved jigsaw puzzles and books. He was also very musical and always wanted the drum during band sessions. His favourite song was

> "I can play on the big bass drum
> And this is the way we do it.
> Boom, boom, boom goes the big bass drum
> There is nothing to it.
> I can play on the violin
> And this is the way we do it
> Fiddle dee dee on the violin
> There is nothing to it",

and then ting, ting, ting on the triangle and toot, toot toot on the silver flute.

Many years later I met their aunt who told me Stanley was now a physical training instructor in the army. Victor was married with a baby girl and worked in the local library. He played in a band at weekends but guitar, not on the big bass drum.

After my exciting experience during Festival week, I stayed friends with Vicki Barter our chaperone and regularly babysat for a neighbour of hers. Mr and Mrs Brozak had separated but each Tuesday they went out together whilst I looked after their nine year old daughter Janina. She was a dear little girl. We had our tea together and she was meant to have a strict 7.30 bedtime. We had our big secret! I allowed her to stay up until 8 o'clock to listen to George Cole (Arthur in "Minder") on the wireless in the popular comedy "Life of Bliss" with Percy Edwards as the dog "Psyche."

On Wednesdays I had a meal with Diana Mulloy prior to us both cycling to Red Cross First Aid classes. One day I arrived there and the place was in chaos, clothes everywhere drying, or being sorted. Her husband Eddie told me this story.

He came from a town in the Scottish Highlands and had taken the family back to his home for the summer holidays. This involved changing trains three times. They arrived, but their luggage didn't. Fortunately they were insured so they had to buy new clothing. That very morning the cases had turned up having been sent to Jamaica! The hold of the ship they had been returned in had let in water and everything was sodden. The insurance company sent them back to them to salvage what they could, hence all the confusion. They were actually able to use many of the items, although the suitcases were useless, so the story ended happily.

I had kept in touch with Mrs Cooper after Godfrey left and bought my fruit and vegetables there each week. I often stopped and shared a cup of tea with her. I did not need to do much catering at home as I ate my main meal midday. Eggs on toast or baked beans on toast seemed to be my main diet, as well as fruit which I have always enjoyed. At Christmas I ordered a box of fruit from Mrs Cooper as a Christmas gift for the Mulloys and a box for Diddley's family. When I collected them Mrs Cooper asked if I was busy on the evening of December 29th, as she was having a Christmas party. I am not really a "party" person, preferring to be with people individually or in a very small group. I think that the Festival week experience had gone to my head and I felt a bit reckless. Why not? I thought, little knowing it would be the catalyst that would change my life.

Mrs Cooper had invited me to the party to even up the numbers. She was friendly with Will Solomon, a captain in the R.E.M.E. (Royal Electrical and Mechanical Engineers) stationed at Guildford and his wife Win. Win's brother, Don Day, was spending Christmas with the family so she had invited him also. I remember not enjoying the party, as they played some embarrassing games. It was a bitterly cold night and Will kindly offered to give me a lift home in his car, leaving my bike there. I think Don felt as ill at ease as I had at the party. He was quite a bit older than the boys I had been going out with. At thirty his hair was definitely greying. He asked to take me out, but I told him I had a boyfriend, so that was that — (for the time being).

Win discovered I loved children and was delighted to have a reliable babysitter. Valerie was then eleven and Stephen four. When I bathed him, he said "Don't look at me while I take off my vest, it's RUDE."

I could bathe him with no clothes on! Now a successful solicitor, I reminded him of this story not long ago, to his great embarrassment.

Quite a while later when, as well as babysitting, I had become a friend of the family, Win and Will took me as a treat to a London theatre to see a revue. They needed a babysitter whilst they took out their babysitter! Win couldn't bear to have a bachelor brother and I was then without a boyfriend.

She'd invited Don, who lived in Chingford, the other side of London, to join us and stay for the weekend. That was how I re-met my future husband.

CHAPTER
TWELVE

A Roman Catholic I became, baptised by Father Price.
He gave me wise instruction and also good advice.

I was born to Jewish parents, my paternal grandfather
having been Rabbi of Dover for fifty years. As a small
child I was brought up in the Jewish faith. I went to
twelve different schools of various denominations, and
was influenced by the various families with whom I
lived, Presbyterian, Church of England and Roman
Catholic. I felt a strong affinity to the latter. I knew
legally one could change one's religion at eighteen. I
went to the local priest in Guildford, Father John Price
and asked him to instruct me in the Faith.

"Have you your father's permission?" he asked.

"No," I admitted.

"Well come back when you are twenty one," he said,
to my great disappointment. I knew I could wait and
would not change my mind. I would often joke and say
I was a better Catholic before I became one.

The famous Catholic Nursing Home run by the
Franciscan Missionaries of the Divine Motherhood,
called Mount Alvernia, was situated on the hill in
Guildford. Hilaire Belloc died there. I passed it each

day as I cycled from Harvey Road to St Luke's Hospital. Whenever my shifts allowed, I attended Mass in the charming chapel.

I was well over twenty one when I started on my six months instruction, the delay due to my hip operation. To my great joy I was baptised at Easter 1953 at St Joseph's Church, Guildford, Diddley being one of my godmothers and schoolfriend Maureen, the other.

Afterwards we celebrated with tea in Fullers tea rooms and went to the pictures to see "Genevieve", that wonderful film about the London to Brighton car race that has become a classic. Kenneth More was always a favourite of mine.

I received weekly guidance from Father Price, an excellent teacher. "Remember to thank God every day," was one piece of advice he gave me. Many of the Catholic fundamentals I knew from my schooldays. Those were the days before "Vatican II" when children learned their Catechism from the little red book and recited it verbatim, often having little idea of the meaning. I remember the first questions in the book.

"Who made you?"

"God made me."

"Why did God make you?"

"God made me to know him, love him, serve him in this world and be happy with him forever in the next."

When I was a child at a Catholic convent, expressions mystified me. In a litany we chanted —

"Blessed be St Joseph, her most chaste spouse."

I wondered why Our Lady was chasing St Joseph! The
other phrase was —

> "Sweet Heart of Jesus, we thee implore,
> Oh make us love Thee more and more."

In all our gospel readings, no reference was made to
Jesus having a sweetheart!

The only person who confirmed parishioners was the
Bishop who visited rarely. After I had been received
into the Church I lived in Great Bookham, so my
Confirmation took place at Effingham with Diddley,
Jock and their three children attending. Dan Maloney
gave me a lovely leather Latin missal which I have still
and sadly is only of use as a memento.

The Mass is no longer in Latin and the priest now
faces the congregation. Many other changes have taken
place but the Eucharist is still basically the same. I
have always felt very blessed that I had the opportunity
to step forward in my beliefs. That is how I see it with
my Jewish background. My Faith has been an
enormous source of strength, joy and consolation to
me, all of my life.

CHAPTER
THIRTEEN

With Mrs Carter's children I explored the Surrey lanes,
We picked the sweet wild strawberries and made
  our daisy chains.

At weekends and often on my days off during my
nursing days I visited Diddley and I was always sure of
a warm welcome. Diddley, real name Pat, was the
sister of Dan Maloney with whom I had boarded for
many years. Christmases had always been spent at
Diddley and Jock's home when all the extended family,
including me, got together. I am happy to say, I am
still thought of as part of the family with "Diddley's
kiddleys!" She and Jock were parents to Veronica,
Angela and Ian. I loved them all.
  A little story concerns them whilst living in
Littlehampton where Jock taught at the time. The two
little girls, probably aged about seven and five walked
home from school along a lane. They met a man who
exposed himself. Veronica hurried into the kitchen.
  "Mummy," she said, "there was a man in the lane
with his 'thing' sticking out."
  "Was there?" comforted Diddley, wisely distracting
them by giving them a biscuit and asking about school.

A short while later that day she chatted to some friends, oblivious of the fact that little Ian was present. She discussed the indecent exposure and said, "Veronica said the man had his 'thing' sticking out."

"Yes," agreed the friend "the man must be off his head to do a thing like that to two little girls."

Later when Diddley tucked Ian into bed he said,

"You know that man Mummy."

"What man?" she asked.

"You know, that one that Veronica and Angie saw, I bet he looked funny."

"What DO you mean?" Diddley asked.

"Well, he had his 'thing' sticking out and no head!" Children always take things literally!

When I had finished my relief work at Shepherds Hill Nursery School, I had no immediate plans and Diddley suggested a job for me. She then lived in Great Bookham, half an hour's bus ride from Guildford. Diddley's neighbour, Barbara Carter, wished to return to her job in London and was looking for someone to take care of her three children, Fairclough (known as Clough) aged six, Caroline, five and Ian just four, the same age as Diddley's Ian.

Barbara's husband was a Captain in the Army in Kenya. I suspect he was not returning, as whilst I was there, the children heard nothing from him. I went for an interview and succeeded in getting the job as nanny to the "Carter kids".

I packed up my few belongings from Denzil Road and moved to Great Bookham as a live-in nanny/governess. I had sole charge of the children all week. Clough walked to school each day and Caroline and Ian stayed home. I remember using the Ladybird books to read to them and teach them the elements of reading. Caroline was a bright little girl. For sums we used precious Smarties. (Sweets were still rationed.) They each had two groups of five. We did simple additions and ALWAYS ended with subtraction until there were none left!

One day to my surprise, I received a parcel with "Return to Sender" stamped on it. Imagine my astonishment when I found it contained the now rather sticky peppermint lumps that I had sent to Bill months earlier. We didn't care if they weren't in "mint" condition! We really enjoyed this bonus.

We went for walks in the fields of the beautiful Surrey countryside, leisurely making daisy chains or picking buttercups. Ian Campbell, Diddley's son, often accompanied us. The two little boys disposed of a lot of their excess energy kicking a ball, reluctantly allowing Caroline to join them. Sometimes we strolled up Rectory Lane and picked the tiny, sweet wild strawberries. The area is so unspoiled that they grow there still. We walked past the School of "Witchery and Vice", this being the local nickname of the School of Stitchery and Lace for Cripples. (Now known as The Grange.) The women, all in wheelchairs, produced exquisite work.

We often went into the woods to pick bluebells or just for a "nature walk" and returned with all sorts of interesting items, sprouting acorns, pebbles, colourful

84

toadstools, and if we went prepared with matchboxes, insects. When we came home we displayed our treasures and had a discussion about them. I was emphatic about hand washing as so many fungi are very poisonous.

I gave the children lunch and did the shopping. We ate high tea together when Mrs Carter returned. A favourite savoury spread of the children's, similar to Vegemite or Marmite, was called Betox. Ian always referred to it as "peacocks". Imagine the grocer's consternation when I innocently asked for a "jar of peacocks"! That quaint shop is there still.

Ian was quite a greedy little boy and like to pile his plate high with his favourite pudding, treacle tart.

"No Ian," I admonished, "no more, if you have any more it will be TOO much."

He then would stamp his little feet and demand "I want TOO much, give me TOO much!!" (Another catchphrase in our home.)

Naturally I saw a lot of Diddley and family which delighted me. At weekends Don came to take me out. His motorbike was very different from Tony's which befitted a more mature man. It was all silver, an L.E. Velocette, almost silent. This model was commonly used by the Police Force probably because of its quietness and reliability. The children loved Don's visits, especially Caroline of whom he was particularly fond. Our second daughter was named after her. I was very flattered that this older, much wiser man was interested in me.

After going out with Tony, initials M.A.N., I graduated to palindromic D.A.D. — Donald Albert Day — (birthday too, 22.11.22). I knew Don had been a Bomb Aimer, flying in Lancasters during the war but he spoke very little about it. Years later I discovered he was in 617 Squadron, the famous Dam Busters. Both his parents died when he was eleven and he and his younger sister became wards of his Aunt Ede. They still lived with her in Chingford, North East of London.

One day poor Clough was not at all well, but Mrs Carter walked off briskly to the station as usual to catch the train to London. The poor little boy's condition deteriorated during the day. I took the initiative of calling the doctor. He was most concerned and said he feared it was pneumonia and advised admitting him to hospital. Naturally I phoned Mrs Carter and asked her to return. She coldly asked me, "Is it really necessary? I still have business to conduct here."

Her reply appalled me. She seemed more concerned with her work than her son. Clough recovered after a short hospital stay, but I decided to give Mrs Carter two weeks' notice.

CHAPTER
FOURTEEN

Serving in a shop is what I thought I'd never do,
Selling skirts and jumpers and those umbrellas too.

I had absolutely no idea where I would live or what I would do. Diddley made me endless cups of tea and together we perused the "Surrey Advertiser". I found a room to let, in Agraria Road, not far from the Royal Surrey County Hospital. By now, a year later, the pain from my hip had greatly improved but I still walked with a pronounced limp. I knew I could not return to nursing yet. (As it happened, I never did.)

"Here's a job for you," she said, "Trained Nursery Nurse wanted for Day Nursery in Camberley."

"Oh no," I argued, "that's much too far away!"

Each post seemed to be unsuitable for some reason. Then she said, "Here's something different, how do you feel about working in a shop?"

Actually, I had always hated the idea, it was almost as bad as working in an office, the bottom of my list. I needed to work, so reluctantly thought I might try it.

"I hope it is not a shop in Camberley," I answered facetiously.

"No," replied Diddley, "they are asking for assistants in 'Whites', you know, the big department store in Guildford High Street."

"All right," I said, "I don't think I will cope there for long, but it will do for the time being."

Although I had no experience I presumed I would be accepted, and I was.

A family owned business dating back to 1799, Whites retained its old fashioned standards and atmosphere. "Be respectful to your elders and betters!" When portly, white haired Mr White perambulated throughout the store, it was very similar to "young Mr Grace" in the TV programme *Are You Being Served?*

Some of the staff lived in. The hostel was behind the shop over the work-room where clothes alterations were carried out. I believe the housekeeper was a real old harridan, very strict, insisting on a curfew at 10p.m. Some of the girls were only fourteen as that was the school leaving age. They came from outlying villages and I am sure it was good for the parents to know that their daughters were cared for. Our uniform was a plain black dress and plain black shoes summer and winter although I was only there in the winter.

The department where I worked sold skirts, jumpers and rather incongruously, umbrellas. How I hated them! The conventional ones were all right, it was the new collapsible ones that infuriated me. Their brand name was GROWY, but could I make the wretched things "grow?" No I could not. I dreaded being asked to demonstrate one.

"Certainly Madam," I said. "I'll show you how easy they are to use."

I went red in the face trying to persuade the spring to release and open the reluctant thing.

"That's seven years' bad luck," muttered superstitious Mavis, a colleague, but one had to oblige the customer.

Surrey was an affluent county and Guildford then the County Town. Many titled and upper class people living in the area were among the clientèle at such a well established store. The buyer for our department, a florid faced, buxom lady, Miss Evans, took each new assistant aside when she arrived on her first day.

"Remembah," she reminded us, "courtesy at ALL taimes, we are heah to serve, and nevah forget the customer is always raight."

"Yes Miss Evans," I answered humbly.

Once she severely chastised me for selling the Countess of Onslow a twelve and sixpenny jumper. She would have bought the most expensive cashmere, had I shown it to her. I had no idea who she was until she asked, "Put it on my account, will you my dear?"

A totally charming lady with no pretensions. At the other extreme was Lady Haverton, a newcomer to the aristocracy. She marched in, loudly proclaiming "Y'know who I am don't you?"
We cringed at each visit. She complained about everything.

"Why don't you have any pink umbrellas in stock? I need one to go with my outfit when I meet the Duke of Norfolk." She also name dropped constantly.

There were no departmental cash registers in those days. When a sale was made I issued an invoice and placed it with the cash or cheque into a small cylindrical container. This was then sent on its way by compressed air to a centralised cashier. The receipt and change returned speedily by the same means. This method was a great improvement on the earlier one. Many shops still had a cashier who sat on a higher level, often the floor above. A small container holding the money suspended on pulleys was catapulted on an overhead line. They were then returned by gravity.

Four chairs spaced around the department were for the comfort of the customers. Many an elderly dowager sank on to one thankfully for a short respite before venturing into the neighbouring millinery department. Whites prided itself on the superiority and quantity of its hats. Ladies came from all over Surrey to visit this prestigious display.

I did not enjoy the servility, the atmosphere or the low wages I received as a junior assistant. The best part of my brief time at Whites was meeting Mrs Callum. After Miss Evans, she was the senior assistant, as tall and elegant as Miss Evans would have liked to be! I often collected her bread from the local baker and as he saw me he chuckled, "I know, you want the long loaf for the long lady!"

She and her husband lived in the village of Puttenham, some distance from Guildford. Dick collected her after work each afternoon and occasionally invited me to join them. I loved their home. No "mod cons", they cooked and heated the very old cottage with an efficient Aga solid fuel stove, oil was used for lighting, but I think they DID have running water. They tended their large garden lovingly. No formality, just large curving beds of herbaceous borders, lavender bushes, rhododendrons and some magnificent trees including my favourite, the horse chestnut.

One day Barbara Callum and I were having a little grumble about Miss Evans' pernicketyness when Dick said, "Eve, you're always saying you don't like shop work, how do you feel about a change?" I brightened up immediately.

"What do you suggest?" I asked.

He was employed by the Ministry of Food and explained that a large new department was opening shortly dealing with the farmers' subsidies for livestock and produce. The Ministry's complex of buildings were a couple of miles east of where I lived, a long cycle ride.

Mrs Wilcox, my landlady, taught dancing at Farnham Girls Grammar School, which I had attended many years previously. She said Miss Cresswell, the Latin teacher whom I remembered well, also remembered me. It was she who used to say, "It's so easy, you could do it standing on your head waving both feet in the air!"

About fifty men and women thronged in the new empty offices. We were interviewed and then took an aptitude test. Meanwhile I continued at Whites, disliking it more daily. At last the welcome letter arrived. "We are pleased to inform you that as a result of your high score in the maths test you are accepted into our three month intensive comptometer course." Delightedly I handed in my notice with no regrets at all. I knew I would keep in touch with the Callums and so started yet another change of career.

CHAPTER
FIFTEEN

Fashions were changing for boys as well as girls.
Their hair was in a pony tail or waved, no longer curls.

Following the end of the war in 1945, England, like most of the European countries, suffered a period of economic depression. As a result of the devastation caused by bombing, the housing shortage was acute. Clusters of individual prefabricated buildings (pre-fabs) appeared on cleared bomb sites. They were meant to be a temporary measure, but twenty years later many were still in use.

Large country mansions and castles were too costly to keep up, so the country's hereditary aristocracy turned most of them into museums for which the public paid an entry fee. The Royal family too, reluctant to encourage ostentation, decreed there would be no presentation of debutantes at Court for the time being.

Rationing was slowly being phased out. I still needed ration books for meat and the cheese ration consisted of only one ounce per week whilst at the Carters in 1952. It took many years of austerity before the "new era" began in the mid fifties. Restrictions then gradually loosened.

England became heavily urbanised. Many people were employed in the various branches of the flourishing metal industry. Quality vehicles, chemicals and electrical goods were produced and exports boomed. Agriculture became progressively mechanised. No more did one see a man laboriously binding sheaves of wheat, the combine harvester had come to stay.

Newspapers, magazines, cinema and later television used advertisements to persuade people to desire "bigger and better". The consumer boom resulted in credit facilities becoming available and also cheaper goods.

Petrol rationing ended in 1950. It cost about three shillings a gallon. The police tested for drunk drivers by making them walk in a straight line and recite tongue twisters!

Sadly many smaller branch lines of the railways closed. The comprehensive network covering most of Britain was now unhappily severely diminished. This gave rise to the classic film *The Titfield Thunderbolt*, about villagers trying to preserve their local railway.

Foreign travel being severely restricted for many years, films became the vogue. Colour now dominated the industry and some excellent memorable films produced.

There were many that were pre-occupied quite naturally with World War II and its aftermath, such as *The Colditz Story*, *Cockleshell Heroes* with Trevor

Howard, and Richard Todd in *The Dam Busters*, a film which was later to have great relevance in my life. Don took me to see that very masculine actor Jack Hawkins in *The Cruel Sea*. Wet Sundays usually saw us taking refuge at the cinema.

I loved some of the excellent musicals of those days. A few I was fortunate enough to see live on the stage in London; *Annie Get Your Gun*, *Oklahoma*, *Salad Days* and later *My Fair Lady*. Doris Day, that shapely blonde with the sparkling eyes and personality, was always a favourite.

Calamity Jane and *Lullaby of Broadway* bring back happy memories as do the many films featuring Frank Sinatra. I think he must have been at the beginning of the "pop" cult, so many of my friends idolised him. (Recently I met a lady who in her youth had been so besotted with Tommy Steele, that she spent all her pocket money on a bottle of what purported to be his bath water!)

Danny Kaye's versatility and charm never failed to delight me. That classic, *The Secret Life of Walter Mitty* shows him at his best. Much of his material was written by his talented wife, Sylvia Fine. He had a charismatic personality as well as being philanthropic. He did an immense amount of fund raising to help UNICEF.

The *Doctor in the House* series began whilst I lived in Guildford. I just loved them. It was not long since my nursing days and I could identify with the situations. James Robertson Justice, so pompous and Dirk Bogarde as Dr Simon Sparrow were excellently cast.

Adulthood and receiving the "key of the door" was not recognised until one reached twenty one (although in MY case because of my circumstances, I had relative freedom much earlier). Young people were expected to do as they were told and conform. At eighteen, men had two years compulsory National Service in one of the forces, unless for a good reason it was deferred. Many objected to this, but in retrospect, it gave them discipline and new experiences.

Fashions were changing. Synthetic fabrics such as nylon were introduced. Girls started wearing pony tails or else had softly waved hair. (I was fortunate there.) Full skirts were popular but personally I never wore either the padded bras that were the vogue, or high heels. Pantihose had not been invented, instead suspender belts held up our stockings.

Christian Dior introduced the "New Look" in 1947. A feminine shape was now in vogue. Rounded bosoms and hips, a tiny waist and full petticoated skirts only twelve inches from the ground.

Some of the more trendy young men were called "teddy boys" and wore velvet collars, string ties, suede shoes with crêpe rubber soles and drainpipe trousers. Boys did not wear "longs" (long trousers) until they reached thirteen. Shorts must have been pretty chilly in an English winter.

The new brighter colours extended to the home, where they replaced many of the drab brown and greens of the forties. The black telephone had a dial and handle on the set. BBC was the only channel available on television and even the radio had only two stations, although sometimes one could fiddle with the knob and get Radio Luxembourg. I remember being delighted one winter's day, unexpectedly hearing Frank Sinatra singing.

> "The snow is snowing,
> The wind is blowing,
> But I will weather the storm.
> What do I care
> How much it may storm?
> I've got my love to keep me warm!"

His songs were immensely popular and he was possibly the first star to have girls swooning when he appeared.

Youngsters were being referred to as "teenagers" for the first time. Advertising had created this phenomenon, persuading them that they needed certain clothing (jeans were not yet in vogue), to buy specific magazines and particularly pop records.

Guy Mitchell's many lighthearted songs are unforgettable.

> "Feet up, pat him on the popo, let's hear him laugh"

and

> "She wears red feathers and a huli huli skirt,
> She wears red feathers and a huli huli skirt
> She lives on just coconuts and fish from the sea . . ."

We loved the Ink Spots —

 "I love coffee, I love tea,
 I love the Java Jive and it loves me . . ."

Jiving was becoming very popular in this era of Rock
and Roll. I could not participate, as I still limped badly
and in any event Don didn't dance.

CHAPTER
SIXTEEN

A holiday at Parracombe, poor Lynmouth was a mess.
Outings every Sunday. Don's approval by Aunt Bess.

On most Sundays when the weather was reasonable we
went out for the day on Don's motor bike. He had a
50 mile (80 kms) journey from Chingford to
Guildford, before we started. Often we went to the
South Coast visiting some of the attractive seaside
resorts such as Littlehampton, Eastbourne and
Worthing. Hampton Court, built by Cardinal Wolsey
in 1514, King Henry VIII's favourite country home
was a favourite of ours too. Many a Sunday in summer
we admired the superb landscaped gardens and visited
the stately, fascinating Palace. The Botanical Gardens
at Kew were nearby with an abundance of floral
displays, shady walks and the great glass Palm House.
We made a dash for this, or one of the many
greenhouses, when caught in a shower.
　We went for a week's holiday in North Devon
staying at Parracombe, a quaint little village, in a lovely
old stone house, one of many "Lorna Doone" farms on
Exmoor, some having been used in films. I remember
stopping near that famous Bronze Age site,

Stonehenge, while Don made some adjustments to the motor bike. When we stopped, the field was full of scattered black and white cattle. Before we left, maybe twenty minutes later, ALL of them were lined up, heads over the fence watching us! There were some beautiful walks on Exmoor and up to Countisbury Hill. The views from there enchanted me. We could see the wooded Watersmeet Valley, and look down on ill fated Lynmouth.

Two years previously in 1952, one of the most violent storms ever to hit Britain centred on this small picturesque coastal town. The torrential floods destroyed a hundred houses, many were washed out to sea, thirty one people died. The tragedy was that because of its isolated position with the steep roads and many bridges washed away, help was unable to arrive for some time. When we visited Lynmouth a considerable amount of rebuilding was taking place.

Sometimes when we went for a ride on a really cold winter's day, I would be so cold when I dismounted the motor bike, I stayed literally frozen in that ungainly legs apart position until I thawed!

Occasionally I met Don in London. The meeting place was always the steps of the National Gallery in Trafalgar Square. This was not far from the Strand where Don was employed as senior technician in the Mechanical Engineering department of King's College. We ate at the Quality Inn Restaurant in Leicester Square and usually I had a toasted three decker sandwich followed by a waffle with maple syrup. Don has always said of my appetite, that it was a relief to take out a girl who ATE and didn't toy with her food! Sometimes we saw a film or went to a show. He introduced me to his great love, opera, by taking me to Sadlers Wells Theatre. There they were sung in English. It was an excellent introduction for me to learn to appreciate the quality productions he took me to later at Covent Garden. These were sung in the language in which they had been written.

During September in 1954 we intended to spend the day at Arundel in Sussex. The Duke of Norfolk, the Earl Marshal of England, lived in the castle of this ancient town. One of "Diddleys kiddleys" once said "I know who lives there, the Norf of Dufolk," yet one more catchphrase. He is always referred to by us as "the Norf".

As we were setting off early on the Sunday morning, to my surprise Don proposed to me. I said "yes" but was so dumbfounded I was practically silent all the way to Sussex, unheard of! The next Saturday we found a ring I liked. (Not at Walter Joseph's.) I have always preferred pre-loved jewellery and semi-precious stones. We found an attractive garnet ring that fitted me, then we met Dad to tell him the news. He seemed to be pleased, but immediately suggested we went to visit Aunt Bess, his elder sister, in Eastbourne so that she could meet (and approve of) Don.

The matriarch of the family, she had no children of her own. She married Uncle Bob, her second husband, a handsome Canadian doctor, after Walter Joseph died. In spite of being born with a withered arm and losing all her hair when young, she lived to be a hundred and one. I called her my "Wiggy Aunt" because of her obvious yellow wig. Visiting her when she must have been ninety eight, I dared to ask her, "How old are you now, Auntie?" to have the curt reply, "You don't ask a lady her age!"

I duly took Don there for lunch for the official "approval"! First she entertained us in the drawing room still decorated as it would have been in Victorian times. (As a small child I had been convinced its name was because I sat at a small table there, DRAWING!)

Everything about Aunt Bess and their lovely home was very refined. Words such as "lavatory" (we never used "toilet") were far too common.

Before we adjourned to the dining room on the lower floor, she asked solicitously, "Does Don know where to go if he wants to 'be a lady?'"! (her euphemism for the lavatory!) I could have told her . . .

When this ordeal was over, we made plans to marry the following March. I had already been to Chingford and met Don's younger sister Gwen and Aunt Ede and Uncle John with whom she was still living. His Aunt Gladys and Uncle Arthur lived four doors away. He had two other uncles who lived close by in Walthamstow; Uncle Bert and Uncle Ernie. Uncle Ernie's eldest daughter Evelyn, then a ten year old, was eventually sponsored by us in 1971. Now known as Eve, she and her husband Mac joined us with their young family here in Australia and she became my closest friend.

Don's great friend Sid, his wife Rita and little girl Valerie often met us on our Sunday outings. They boasted a motor bike with a sidecar, a popular means of transport in those days. Once when we visited Bognor and had enjoyed an ice cream cornet, Valerie, aged about two, ran up to Rita, "Mummy, 'ook 'ands 'ticky," showing us her sticky fingers.

Facetiously Rita muttered, "Go and wipe them on Uncle Don"s trousers then."

She did!

CHAPTER
SEVENTEEN

At the Ministry of Food, I had my choice between
Working with comptometers or Hollerith machine.

My new job at the Ministry of Food was with the
"Computing Machine Training School" where I
learned to become a Comptometer Operator. The
training was very intensive and made far more difficult
as we were not metric. The electric machine was a
similar size to a typewriter with rows of numbers, 0-10.
As well as knowing our Imperial measurements
accurately, we also had to convert everything to
decimals. To this day, one of the many useless pieces
of information embedded in my mind, is that .00416
recurring is one penny as a decimal of one pound. We
also did a lot of work with reciprocals (the answer
obtained by dividing the number "into one") and
converting fractions into decimals. This course was
not easy as it was so concentrated. Only about half of
us passed the exam the first time. Then we had the
choice, to remain and work in the Comptometer Pool
or join the "élite" in the new department dealing with
subsidies for farmers, using Hollerith machines.

I opted for the latter. I had always disliked the thought of sitting in an office.

Prior to the computer as we know it, or even before the silicon chip, when it was a huge machine, basic operations were performed using electric readings of punched cards. The two major operators were Hollerith and Powers-Samas. The Ministry of Food used the Hollerith method. The cards were colour coded according to subject. Pigs — blue, live sheep — pink, dead sheep — brown, dead cattle — grey and so on. Each card had eighty columns across and nine down.

Various machines were used, all electrically operated. The Puncher transferred information from the farmers' forms to a card that the machine could read. We used a special "alpha" code. The sorter sorted the cards to whatever column was relevant. The Gang Puncher punched common information on to blank or partly punched cards such as the same breed of pig, or the same weight. It punched a hundred cards a minute, but had to be checked frequently for errors by "needle checking", poking a long metal needle through the relevant hole.

These methods were quite innovative then, but seem positively prehistoric now. My friend Jean worked on the Tabulator dealing with listing, control card distribution and selection. I spent some time on most of these machines, but ended up on the Reproducer. Here we stood at a machine about four feet high. The cards had to be joggled carefully, to ensure smooth feeding and stacking. We set up the machine to reproduce common information, such as district and prices. I worked with an uninspiring little man called George. The two of us spent everyday reproducing and I have a photo to prove it!

We had an active Social Club. Mr Worsfold the head of our department was a kind and very approachable man. He arranged occasional outings at weekends. We had excellent subsidised canteen facilities and the pay was good. I had never envisaged myself doing such work but life is full of surprises.

CHAPTER
EIGHTEEN

At Don's sister's on TV we watched the Coronation.
Although it rained, it did not quell the nation's jubilation.

By the time Don and I became engaged, his sister Win
had taken the children to join Will, who was stationed
in Sierra Leone. She did not have the satisfaction of
attending the wedding she had hoped for. Prior to her
departure we visited her often and Don sometimes
stayed overnight with them.

One rainy day I spent with them I shall never forget
— the second of June 1953, the Queen's Coronation.
As Ian Coster wrote, "it was a triumph of colour over
climate, of pageantry over pessimism". I have always
LOVED pageantry. I remember my nanny taking me
to see the Changing of the Guard as a small child,
when we lived in London. Win was one of the few
people I knew who owned a television. The squat,
bulky set had the place of honour in the sitting room
that blustery day as we watched, enamoured, from the
comfort of our armchairs.

The TV cameras filmed the procession all along the
route from Buckingham Palace to Westminster Abbey
(there were no cars at all); down the Mall, Piccadilly,
Park Lane, Oxford Street, Regent Street, Trafalgar

Square and the Embankment. Someone told me later it was almost a trip around the Monopoly board. (That game was popular even in those days.) Everywhere there were Union Jacks — bunting in red, white and blue, heraldic symbols on the lamp posts and a great air of festivity in spite of the inclement weather.

The Lord Mayor of London headed the parade in his fairy tale coach guarded by the colourful Pikemen. The Household Cavalry with their glossy black horses and wearing plumes in their helmets followed. The Army, Navy and Air Force all in their full regalia looked magnificent. Winston Churchill gave everyone his famous V sign as he rode in a carriage with his elegant wife Clementine.

The honoured Generals and men who had distinguished themselves in the war followed the Prime Ministers from the Dominions. Someone who was admired by us all, was Queen Salote of Tonga with her big smile. She braved the unpredictable English weather by riding in an open carriage. I remember a rhyme in the paper —

"Linger longer, Queen of Tonga,
Linger longer wiv us.
Linger while the English summer
Gives us all the shivers!"

All through this parade silver and brass bands played rousing patriotic music. The kilted Irish and Scots regiments marched, accompanied by bagpipes. Then came the Queen herself in the gilded State Coach drawn by eight grey horses. The huge crowd jostled for an opportunity to see her amid deafening cheers.

The cameras then entered the nine hundred year old Westminster Abbey where two thousand privileged guests waited for this historic event. What a magnificent setting! The Bishops in their copes, the Peers of the Realm in full regalia, the colours contrasting with the grey of the ancient stone. The tension built and as the Queen entered wearing a shimmering dress, everyone stood in silence. The service took two hours.

Win served us food and drink as we chatted to the background of the choirs in the Abbey and only stopped to listen as Queen Elizabeth II, our new sovereign, took the Oath. She wore a simple white dress having been disrobed of her finery and diadem. Then she was dressed in a robe of royal cloth of gold and given the Orb and Sceptre. The Archbishop of Canterbury held the ancient crown of St Edward over her before placing it on her head. The whole Abbey resounded with "GOD SAVE THE QUEEN". It was then that the Peers and Peeresses were allowed to don their coronets. Little four year old Prince Charles behaved admirably sitting with his grandmother the Queen Mother. Princess Anne, not quite two, appeared later when the Royal Family waved to the thousands of enthusiastic well wishers from the balcony at Buckingham Palace. All along the Mall illuminations had been switched on and the happy crowds spent an evening celebrating and rejoicing.

The news flashed on to the screens that Sir Edmund Hillary had conquered Everest, we all cheered. I heard later that his triumphant Nepalese companion Tenzing Norgay proclaimed, "We done the bugger!"

We didn't see the televised fireworks as Guildford had its own display to celebrate this historic event. Will drove us all to Stoke Park. We huddled in our mackintoshes and oooo'd and ah'd at the colourful spectacle. I love fireworks! What a memorable day!

CHAPTER
NINETEEN

A traditional white wedding — but no promise to obey.
The service and reception, then I became — Eve Day.

Now that I had a ring on my finger I told the happy
news of my engagement to all my friends and relations.
A party never occurred to me and I certainly had no
spare money to indulge in such frivolities. All the same,
I decided I wanted a "proper" wedding, a white
wedding in church with all the paraphernalia that
is involved.

I had only ever been to one wedding. That was Aunt
Toppie's son Derrick who married Yvonne, a Scottish
girl, at a London Synagogue. The reception was a very
grand affair at the Savoy Hotel. My brother David had
bought me a new dress for the occasion, green and
white. (I had it for years and years.) I was acutely
embarrassed when the Master of Ceremonies
announced me, "MISS EVE BARNSTON" he
boomed. I slunk into the room alone as all heads
turned to see the latest unaccompanied arrival.
Anything to do with food always stays in my memory
and the wedding breakfast was exceptional.

At our wedding there could be no Nuptial Mass for two reasons. Firstly we were marrying during Lent and secondly my fiancé was not a Catholic. Don and I had to participate in a series of marriage preparation talks with Father Price, the priest who had received me into the Church a few years earlier. Don promised not to interfere with me practising my religion and that any children would be brought up as Catholics and attend Catholic schools. He kept his promise.

One valuable piece of advice I have always remembered given to me by Father Price, was "NEVER say I told you so". (Two stipulations Don gave me were NEVER to offer him minced meat in ANY form or to give him re-heated food!)

We decided to marry on a Wednesday as it was early closing day in Guildford. Initially my father was not going to give me away. He made the excuse that he couldn't leave the shop on a Saturday but actually I think the reason was that entering a church was so alien to a rabbi's son. Don asked Sid to be his best man and I had always hoped to have two bridesmaids. I asked Geraldine, Mrs Maloney's youngest daughter, but she could not attend that day. Diddley's daughter Angela my other choice agreed but who to have to join her? A middle aged lady I worked with who married late, had an only child, Susan. Mrs Norris always longed for her to have the excitement of being a bridesmaid and willingly had the outfit made for her. The two little girls were both nine years old. Their dresses were turquoise with maroon sashes, head dress of maroon roses and meant to have maroon shoes. (Susan wore her white sandals.)

I saved my babysitting money in a special account for years and decided to use it to pay for the wedding. It was not a lot and I was grateful when a girl at work's sister offered to lend me her wedding dress and veil. I DID buy new shoes and pay for the freesias and lily of the valley bouquet I carried. The bridesmaids had posies of colourful anemones. No flowers were allowed to decorate the church during Lent. The magnificent three tier wedding cake was made by Mrs Cooper at whose house we originally met. She gave it to us as a most welcome gift.

I still lived in my bedsitting room in Agraria Road prior to the wedding. I possessed a few useful artefacts to start married life, such as a folding card table (which I still have), iron and ironing board and cooking utensils. A friend of Don's arranged to come and collect these and take them over to our new "home". Accommodation was not easy to find. We had no capital, so were very grateful when Don's Aunt Gladys and Uncle Arthur offered to rent us one of the bedrooms in their small house in Chingford. We lived, ate, and cooked and slept in that one room 12 feet by 10 feet.

Nick's mother was horrified that I would be going to the church alone. "A girl needs a fuss made of her before her wedding day," she insisted. She had no daughters of her own and was extremely kind to me. She invited me to stay the night and as the ceremony was not until 3 o'clock asked me, "What you would like for lunch, anything you fancy?"

I had never been so indulged.

"Chicken please," I replied, a real treat in those days. I was disappointed that her husband had recently sold his Rolls Royce but he now had an elegant car, a Jowett Javelin. He chauffeured me to the church and the reception. Nick and Ambrose were groomsmen.

The day of the wedding was freezing cold, it even snowed in the morning. The blustery weather sadly prevented a couple of elderly relatives from attending. The service at St Joseph's Catholic church was the brief wedding service followed by the signing of the legal documents. The professional photographer took the photos fairly quickly, as everyone was shivering.

The Prince of Wales hotel was the venue for our afternoon buffet meal and usual necessary speeches. I paid for this and recently I found the bill, totalling less than seventeen pounds. Friends and relations proved most generous and we received many wedding gifts including some welcome cheques. One gift I particularly treasure from my mother's cousin, dear Aunt Chris, was a Georgian silver sugar sifter (what a tongue twister!), a magnificent design. Don admired it and twisted it to see how it opened. Imagine our surprise and delight to find a five pound note tucked inside, a lot of money in those days. Occasionally we tried opening it again to see if it had produced any more!

When Aunt Bess married Walter Joseph in Dover in 1902 the local paper produced a full page report on the wedding. Her father, the Rabbi of Dover, officiated. Details of the service were given, plus a description of the one hundred and thirty four wedding gifts. "The numerous and costly presents were set out, the whole of which were of exceptional beauty and intrinsic worth." It makes fascinating reading.

The bride gave the bridegroom a gold mounted walking stick. They received such treasures as a Dresden centrepiece, Doulton breakfast set, silver card trays and gold mounted umbrella. Some things are outlandish to us today; cut glass épergne, a worked toilet cover (no, not for the lavatory! but to decorate the dressing table when the lady performs her toilet!) seltsogene, a hall gong and a palm stand.

The wedding presents Don and I received were of a far more modest nature, although the cheques we received gave us a small financial boost to start our married life. I had used all my savings on the wedding. We received strictly utilitarian presents, towels, pillowcases, pyrex casseroles, even a pair of kitchen scissors that I still have. Uncle Manny allowed me to choose a canteen of cutlery from the shop. The girls at work gave me the big Good Housekeeping Cookery book as I was totally ignorant of domesticity. Two of my nursing friends clubbed together to buy me a jam spoon.

How trifling these gifts seem to the extravagant presents expected at weddings these days.

After the reception I changed into my "going away" outfit of grey and bright green. We caught the train for our honeymoon and there I was on the 9th March 1955, no longer Eve Barnston but Mrs Eve Day and a new life ahead of me, what would EVEntuate?

ISIS publish a wide range of books in large print, from fiction to biography. Any suggestions for books you would like to see in large print or audio are always welcome. Please send to the Editorial Department at:

ISIS Publishing Ltd.
7 Centremead
Osney Mead
Oxford OX2 0ES
(01865) 250 333

A full list of titles is available free of charge from:
Ulverscroft Large Print Books

(UK)
The Green
Bradgate Road, Anstey
Leicester LE7 7FU
Tel: (0116) 236 4325

(Australia)
P.O Box 953
Crows Nest
NSW 1585
Tel: (02) 9436 2622

(USA)
1881 Ridge Road
P.O Box 1230, West Seneca,
N.Y. 14224-1230
Tel: (716) 674 4270

(Canada)
P.O Box 80038
Burlington
Ontario L7L 6B1
Tel: (905) 637 8734

(New Zealand)
P.O Box 456
Feilding
Tel: (06) 323 6828

Details of **ISIS** complete and unabridged audio books are also available from these offices. Alternatively, contact your local library for details of their collection of **ISIS** large print and unabridged audio books.

A ZigZag Path
Elizabeth Bowtell

Elizabeth Bowtell's childhood was full of simple pleasures, rummaging through sea-shore rock pools with other carefree children, strolling through flower-carpeted meadows and walking down the narrow alleys of Cornish fishing ports.

Her tale begins and ends in Padstow but the zigzag path she's followed through life led her through the Blitz, to RAF Bomber Stations, Military Intelligence and to Europe, soon after the guns fell silent. With tears and laughter, Elizabeth reflects on her life's joys and hardships, her discovery of love and her patriotic duty and loyalty.